Make Your Move . . .

And Make the Most of Your Life

Make Your Move . . .

And Make the Most of Your Life

Jimmy Calano

John Wiley & Sons, Inc.

Published by John Wiley & Sons, Inc., Hoboken, New Jersey.
Published simultaneously in Canada.

For general information on our other products and services, or technical support, please contact our Customer Care Department within the United States at 800-762-2974, outside the United States at 317-572-3993 or fax 317-572-4002.

Wiley also publishes its books in a variety of electronic formats. Some content that appears in print may not be available in electronic books. For more information about Wiley products, visit our web site at www.wiley.com.

Library of Congress Cataloging-in-Publication Data:

Calano, James.
Make your move—and make the most of your life / Jimmy Calano.
p. cm.
Includes index.
ISBN-13 978-0-471-71637-2
ISBN-10 0-471-71637-5 (cloth)
1. Success—Psychological aspects. 2. Self-actualization (Psychology) I. Title.
BF637.S8C275 2005
650.1—dc22

2004027958

Printed in the United States of America.

10 9 8 7 6 5 4 3 2 1

For Deborah
My toughest critic,
My biggest fan

Contents

PREFACE		ix
ACKNOWLEDGMENTS		xv
Chapter ONE	Harvesting Your Bonus Decade	1
Chapter TWO	Making Your Days Count	19
Chapter THREE	Triumphing over Procrastination	45
Chapter FOUR	Making Things Happen	67
Chapter FIVE	Dusting Off Your Dreams	87
Chapter SIX	Nourishing Your Mind	113
Chapter SEVEN	Rising above the Mean	139
Chapter EIGHT	Dealing with Disappointment	159
AFTERWORD		185
ABOUT THE AUTHOR		189

Preface

In 1982, I cofounded the international training company, CareerTrack. By 1992, it had become one of the world's largest purveyors of personal and professional development videotapes, audiotapes, and seminar-style training programs. CareerTrack achieved market leadership with its breakthrough instructional formats, affordable tuition fees, and unconventional direct-marketing strategies. The company grew to $82 million in revenue, employed 700 people, and was conducting business in 24 countries. In 1995, after presiding over the company for 13 years, I sold it to a multinational corporation.

At 38 I was suddenly retired with half of my years—more or less—still ahead of me. I literally had the rest of my life to do whatever I pleased. One of those pleasures was writing this book, which is based on speeches I've given, articles I've written, and observations I've made over the past three decades. I offer my personal perspectives on eight subjects: exploiting the bonus decade, making the most of your days, overcoming procrastination, taking initiative, reaching for dreams, learning continuously, rising above mediocrity, and rebounding from setbacks. Essentially, these topics are about creating more and deeper fulfillments in your life, and I believe they fit nicely under the *Make Your Move* umbrella. The content is not simply about motivating you to do more with your life; it is about helping you find the inspiration—and the paths—to do so. Since retiring, I've had ample time to contemplate the impact of these concepts on my own achievements, and on those of the extraordinary people I've known and with whom I've worked.

My former company was dubbed the McDonald's of the continuing education industry. After all, we taught more than one million people annually in subjects ranging from Scott Peck's *The Road Less Traveled* (Touchstone, 1988) to Tom Peters' *In Search of Excellence* (Harper & Row, 1982). Having had a hand in training 10 million people on four continents from 1977 to 1998, I discovered a thing or two about what facilitates practical, effective self-development. In these pages, I share some of the best of what I've learned.

If there's one thing I know after my 25 years in the training industry, it's that people who flourish are, without exception, initiators. They create and exploit their own opportunities. This book promotes the belief that life is too short, and prosperity too possible, to let your talents and unrealized ambitions languish. The topics I cover within are intended to help you take flight and actualize your potential. To that end, I quote a three-word sign in my study, "Do Something Now." It has been my motto for as long as I can remember.

Who I Had in Mind

Although I believe this book holds relevance for all readers, my primary audience includes people who have at least a couple of decades under their belts, yet still have not made their move on their lifelong yearnings. From oldest to youngest, here are the demographic groups that would benefit from *Make Your Move*:

- **End-of-career climbers.** These folks are typically empty nesters in their 60s or beyond. Although they may have achieved professional and financial success, many still have not pursued—or even recently contemplated—their noncareer interests. Having put them on hold or ignored them for decades, they now have the time to rekindle the leisure activities they still think about, but have yet to initiate. *Make Your Move* can be their guidebook.
- **Bored baby boomers.** These are people in their 40s or 50s who are wandering aimlessly, stuck in a rut, or antsy for some kind of change, either professionally or personally (e.g., a new career, hobby, or sport). No longer feeling the passion

they once did, bored boomers are primed for ideas and inspiration that can motivate them to rediscover and recommit to their true aspirations. This book will breathe new life into their stale routines.

- **Thirty-something searchers.** These individuals have been surviving in the real world for 10-plus years but are simply not satisfied with the direction their lives have taken. Something is missing. Somewhere along the line, they took the wrong turn and got lost. *Make Your Move* offers these disenchanted drifters ways to reconnect with what excites them. This book can be the catalyst that propels them toward whatever will make them spring to life.
- **Recent (and not-so-recent) college graduates.** *Make Your Move* is relevant to young adults in their early 20s eager to make their mark in the world, as well as appealing to the later-20s crowd—those who have yet to find their personal inspirational path. Senior undergraduates taking a sales management course at the Leeds School of Business (University of Colorado) found an early manuscript version of this book particularly helpful, saying it inspired them to "create" themselves, not just "find" themselves. As one student wrote, "I think anyone can benefit from reading the book, from the graduate looking ahead to the single parent who wants to escape a dead end."

Make Your Move also speaks to those who have allowed their hopes and desires to be neglected, abandoned, or forgotten altogether. To lose sight of one's aspirations is a shame. This book will help readers reconsider their faded dreams with a fresh eye and recommit to pursuing them with newfound vigor.

How to Approach This Book

I don't suggest you read it all at once. Each chapter should take the average reader approximately 20 minutes to complete, and I advise people to spend at least another 20 minutes contemplating the intellections presented. If you read the book in one sitting, it is unlikely you'll reap its full value. If you tackle one subject per day, however, you'll still get through the material in just over a week—and probably get more out of it. I also urge you to experience it twice; that is, read each piece, then read it again. As you'll discover in Chapter 7, "Rising Above the Mean," the second time through will often yield greater insights than the first.

Each chapter is divided into three parts. I begin with get-your-attention stories and anecdotes, then set forth the rewards for espousing the advocated attitudes and taking the recommended actions, concluding with execution how-tos. To give structure and consistency to my messages, I've followed this format throughout.

Unabashedly, I will tell you that this work is highly prescriptive. Given my "use what you know" mind-set, I could not resist offering suggestions at the end of each chapter on how to make it happen. In some cases, the things-to-try section is the longest. And while I don't expect you to implement every technique and exercise I propose, I do hope you'll embrace at least one per topic.

Throughout my adult years, my personal philosophy has been, "It's not what you know, but what you do with what you know that counts." By following this creed, I've achieved my life and career ambitions up to this point, and I believe this is how most others go about accomplishing theirs. Having knowledge is one thing; being able to apply and administer it is quite another. A mediocre idea well executed often produces a better result than a superb idea poorly implemented.

I've spent my entire career in the personal and professional development field, so even though my formal education was in marketing and my title was CEO, advice giving has been my primary occupation. And honestly, I enjoy dispensing advice—especially when it's sound, proven, and welcome. Nonetheless, don't hesitate to challenge my counsel and substitute your own wisdom. Better yet, e-mail me at jcalano@aol.com with your comments and questions.

Now, allow me to share my thoughts on renewing aspirations and seeing the world fresh again.

Acknowledgments

A big thanks to my editor, Debra Englander, for believing in my manuscript from the beginning.

Toni Knapp, your encouragement was a mainstay of inspiration. You guided my pen, supplied the perfect word when it eluded me, and redirected my writing when it veered off course. Without your reassurance, I doubt I would have continued beyond the first chapter.

Jill Rosati, your proofreading skills are second to none. If these pages are error free, you get the credit. You are a joy to work with and a pro at your craft.

My assistant, Sandra Jonas, was the first person to read every draft (and each chapter had no less than a dozen). Your astute input, savvy suggestions, and over-my-shoulder editing were invaluable and much appreciated.

ACKNOWLEDGMENTS

I am indebted to my trusted readers: Bunny Belanger, Allen Buckner, Bill Capsalis, Steve Carter, Delynn Copley, Bill Flagg, Verne Harnish, Jeff Hoye, Alan Kaplan, Matt Leahy, Rob Lewis, Shawn Mulligan, Anthony Pigliacampo, Mark Richards, Jeff Salzman, Mark Sanborn, Scott Shafer, David Stueber, Nathan Thompson, Tom Trumble, and Jim Warner. Unquestionably, your time spent reading and proffering comments made this a better book.

A special thanks to my friends: Roger Ayan, Brian Craven, David Feilmeier, John Fischer, Jana Greenfield, AJ Kitt, Frank Mazzarella, Rick Nachman, Gordon Page, Robert Purcell, Attila Safari, Dawn Siebel, Kane Webber, and Budd Zuckerman. You were generous to share the experiences and wisdom within.

My two children, Brandon and Carsen, were always understanding when I stole away on nights, weekends, and even some holidays to work on the manuscript. I love you for giving me the time and space to write it.

My parents, Gordon Calano and Loretta Dienst, along with my sister, Robin Brodie, were always ready and willing to review my (sometimes daily) faxed and e-mailed pages. I deeply appreciate your support and encouragement.

Thank you, John Boswell, my literary agent for over two decades, for serving as my personal "French Resistance." Although you challenged nearly everything, your healthy skepticism was more of a motivator than you can know.

Lauren Kell, you pushed me in so many positive ways while shepherding me through the publishing labyrinth. Working with you is a delight.

And finally, a special thanks to the family members, friends, and associates who shared their moving narratives and allowed me to retell them. Your stories represent the soul of this book.

Chapter ONE

Harvesting Your Bonus Decade

A Rare Opportunity

A number of years ago, I was asked to deliver the commencement address to the graduating class of the Leeds School of Business at the University of Colorado (CU), my alma mater. It was a great honor, but due to a previous commitment, I had intended to decline. Just for the heck of it, though, I pulled out a yellow pad and scribbled out what I might have said had I been available to make the presentation. Thirty minutes later, after glancing over the pages I had filled, I canceled my previous engagement and gratefully accepted the invitation.

Having sold my company the previous year, I no longer had regular opportunities—or any opportunities, for that matter—to address people who were obliged to listen to my words. Furthermore, there was no way I was going to relinquish such a singular occasion to influence the minds of a new crop of graduates (including MBAs and PhDs) heading into the real world. Having matriculated from the CU Business School 18 years earlier, I was extremely eager to share what I had learned about life after college.

When I consented to speak, however, I didn't know that more than 4,000 people would be in the audience. Hearing that, and having been told there were approximately 1,000 graduates, I realized I would be speaking to a more diverse group than I had expected. I had forgotten about all the professors, parents, relatives, friends, and well-wishers who would be there, witnessing the ceremony. Consequently, I expanded my message and viewed it as an opportunity to pass on some hard-earned wisdom to everyone in attendance.

The rest of this chapter is an expanded version of the talk I gave at that commencement. While this material may seem more pertinent to those younger than you, I believe it contains universal relevance to people of all ages. Moreover, even if you are well beyond early adulthood, surely you or your friends have children, nieces, nephews, godchildren, or grandchildren who are just now beginning their postcollege days. So if you find something worthwhile in my words, pass it on to the 20-somethings whose future you care about.

A Bit about Me

Let me begin with a brief synopsis of the past few decades of my life, so you'll understand my perspective:

In 1978, I graduated from the CU Business School with a BA (or was it a BS?) in marketing.

By 1979, I was thriving in my first job, which I loved, in an industry that enthralled me.

By 1982, I had already experienced two career "transitions"—that is, I'd been fired twice.

By 1984, along with my partner, Jeff Salzman, I had

built a business that was generating $5 million in revenue and employing 100 people.

By 1992, the company had grown to $80 million in revenue and 700 employees, and was doing business in 24 countries on four continents.

In 1995, my partner and I sold the enterprise for a considerable sum and split the proceeds. At the age of 38, I was retired and financially set, and I had the rest of my life to do whatever I wanted.

Granted, this somewhat braggadocio display of personal prosperity might be off-putting to some of you. Remember, though, I graduated from the Leeds School of Business where students are taught that it's more than okay to make a profit—and be proud of it. Given that my educational roots are similar to yours, I'd like to share what I learned it takes—beyond a sheepskin—to achieve extraordinary levels of accomplishment in life.

After considerable reflection, I came up with several insights and recommendations I believe are worthy of your attention. I warn you, however, that some of the ideas may be unsettling, and at first you may even reject them. Nevertheless, hear them through and see if they do, in fact, resonate with you. Here is my counsel for you to ponder—and then act upon.

The 10-Year Graduation Gift

Did you know that the average life expectancy at the turn of the twentieth century was just 47? The latest government statistics show that in the past hundred years, it has increased by more than 60 percent, or three decades, to 77. In the 1950s, when my generation was born, the expected life span was around 67. Most of you, therefore, will live a decade longer than you would have had you been born 25 years earlier.

In the second half of the twentieth century, modern medicine bestowed on you an incredible gift—10 extra years of life, or, put another way, 15 percent more life to live. I consider your 20s to be that "bonus" decade—a once-in-a-lifetime opportunity to set the stage and establish yourself for the rest of your life. It's an ideal period to explore your options, focus your energies, refine your talents, establish your career, and define yourself. Your 20s provide the space to learn who you are, determine what you stand for, and figure out exactly what life you want to live—*and how you'll live it.* I have found that you learn these things by acting on them, not by thinking about them.

Your 20s are the optimum time to *take* your time making the major decisions of your life, some of which you'll inevitably change. These are decisions such as where you'll live, which career field you'll choose, what advanced degrees you may pursue, who your ideal spouse/significant other will be, and what your family plans will include. These are critical choices you shouldn't rush—and don't have to.

You may feel anxious about what you are facing—that's fine. How else *could* you feel? Many of you have never been out of school! *Don't let this apprehension, though, be a license to coast.* You don't need to consider your choices irrevocable. Instead, make provisional decisions and give them everything you've got. While your peers will be finding themselves as they try to formulate their options, you'll be *creating yourself* in the crucible of real-life experience.

So here are two challenges for you to ruminate on: First, how do you reap the benefits of the education and social skills you've accumulated thus far? Second, how do you apply your academic credentials, along with your natural talents, to add a certain unique value to the world? Well, you don't do it by simply contemplating it. And while some of your peers may want to slow down, take it easy, and not race into anything, I recommend you do precisely the opposite.

This is the time to take flight—to unite all of your life's assets and put them into action. You have the youthful energy, fueled by dreams and determination, to do it. There are rewards for taking advantage of your 20s. I will present them to you now, along with imparting my thoughts on how you can best attain them.

The Advantages of Taking Advantage of Your "Extra 10"

Freedom

If you're a recent college graduate, you've finally got it: no more school, no need to rely on your folks for sustenance, and no dependents of your own—not yet, anyway. Plus, now you have an advanced education, a way to make a good living, and few financial obligations (other than perhaps a college loan you'd like to forget about). You have carte blanche to create your life as you want. Now, *that's* freedom.

Set Yourself Up for Life

If you expend your 20s merely dabbling at this and that, you'll likely fall behind in your life ambitions. Parents, don't we all have friends, relatives, and associates who played too much in their 20s only to pay the price in their 30s and 40s? Trust me on this one: Don't drift from 22 to 30, because if you do, your 30s, 40s, 50s, 60s, and beyond will be far less satisfying and comfortable.

More Time down the Road

As the decades pass, the emphasis you place on your career will inevitably change, in that you'll want to spend more time on other interests besides work. Hobbies, friends, sports, vacations, and a multitude of other activities will invade the time you have—and want—to give to your career. If you give your occupation top priority in your 20s, you'll have ample time to pursue these other interests later on.

You Won't Get Stuck

Ruts are no fun. They hold you back, drag you down, and waste your life. If you sprint out of the academic starting blocks with vigor, you'll be less inclined to stagnate in a dead-end job or become paralyzed by indecision over which career direction to take. Instead, you'll take charge of this new life phase, and make every minute and motion count.

Be a Better Parent

I'm 100 percent certain that I was a better parent in my 30s than I ever could have been in my 20s. I was more mature, financially secure, and fortunate enough to find a mate with whom I wanted to have children. Plus, I had more experience interacting with kids as a result of having been in the Big Brothers program for more than a dozen years. The responsibility of raising children can be taxing, and trying to do it while still in your 20s can be overwhelming. If you can wait to start a family, you'll be able to give it the time, love, and attention everyone deserves.

A Second Chance

For those of you well past your 20s, you, too, have the gift of an extra 10 years—at least compared to the life expectancy of your parents' generation. Many of the precepts that follow are equally germane to your lives, so listen up. It's never too late to put another decade to good use.

The Means for Making Your Third Decade Matter

Know Your Purpose

Around the time I graduated from college, a perceptive mentor posed the most probing question I had ever been asked: What is the purpose of your life? I had to think long and hard before I could reply. I found myself pondering related questions—ones I had never given much thought to, such as: Where can I make an impact? How can I make this world a slightly better place? Why am I here? Who was I meant to become? I suggest you devote time to examining your responses to these life-defining queries. During the ensuing years, your answers will likely become clearer and more profound—they may even surprise you.

Make Consequential Life Decisions As Early As You Can

Eventually, all of us must face these fundamental issues:

- *College* (if yes, local versus out-of-state? campus size? major?)
- *Career* (profession? industry? large or small company?)
- *Living location* (big city or small town?)
- *Marriage* (will you settle down? what are your ideal mate's qualities?)
- *Children* (if yes, optimally, how many and when to start the family?)
- *Financial* (how much will you need for the lifestyle you desire?)
- *Personal interests* (what are your hobbies? passions?)
- *Retirement* (when and where?)

Most people confront the first key decision around age 16. I'd advise contemplating seriously all but the last before your late 20s. Unfortunately, some folks don't choose until their late 30s or beyond, and others never commit, forever rethinking and, thus, upending their lives. The sooner you make these critical calls, the sooner you can begin acting on them. While you don't want to decide in haste, and inevitably you'll make adjustments due to job relocations, relationships, and economics, having a sense of what's right for you early on will serve you well. (Not convinced? If you're over 40, reflect on the impact these decisions have already had on your life.)

Put Your Career First

Begin your postgraduation phase with an absolute sense of urgency about your profession. Consider the next eight years a watershed period—a chance to lay a career foundation that will give you a lifelong advantage. In other words, this is the time—right now—to work hard, sacrifice some good times (I said *some*, not all), and focus your priorities on your professional life.

Don't Dally

You might be groaning at the moment, thinking about what you just went through to complete your degree. Yes, for four-plus years you attended classes religiously (well, some of you did); studied hard (okay, when you could fit studying into your overloaded social calendar); did your advance reading (from time to time, anyway); researched assiduously (all right, when absolutely necessary); wrote and rewrote your papers (with the exception of those last-minute, first-draft submissions); and passed your exams (most of them, anyway). Yet, starting today is when giving your best effort really counts. Until now you've just been paying your academic dues to get in the real game. The time has arrived to pull out the stops, pour it on, and put your scholastic accomplishments to work.

Stay the Course

Once you find the right vocational path, *stay on it*. I look back at my own career and realize I essentially did the same thing from age 19 until I retired. I loved my profession—producing training programs—and it always felt right to me. Along the way, I did fall for occasional "grass is greener" thinking, and I took a few detours that sounded more attractive. But once I figured out that sticking to my knitting was the best plan, I quickly got back on track. Consequently, as the years passed, I was able to refine my skills, better understand my business, and capitalize on my compounding industry knowledge. I stayed the course, and I gave it my all. The dividends for my one-track approach far surpassed my expectations.

Accelerate, but Don't Rush

Why work incredibly hard right off the bat? Because you have the drive, the energy, the enthusiasm, and the optimism, but with few burdensome obligations to distract you. Assuming you are successful, the more you work now, the less you will have to later on. On the other hand, don't charge into the world eager to commit to everything and everyone. Sure, commit all the way to your job and your career, but consider holding back on marriage, kids, and expensive toys. Typically, those things can wait. By taking the time to establish yourself financially, ready yourself emotionally, and ripen your persona, you'll raise the odds of fruitfully launching your adult life. (I do acknowledge, though, that if you meet your soul mate in your early 20s, you may lose that person if you ask him or her to wait a decade.)

Do Your Homework

Just what you wanted to hear, right? Especially after you just finished writing term papers and cramming for finals. Let me explain what I mean by "homework" in the context of a career—it's the nightly processing of your in-box, report writing, idea development, decision analysis, and dealing with paperwork. You get the picture. It's *work* that you literally do *at home*. If there was one activity that gave me a tremendous advantage over my peers and competitors, it was finding and maintaining the discipline to do my homework every night after I graduated. For the past 18 years I did it religiously for three hours most evenings, which is ironic, since I didn't have the willpower to do it for the previous 18 years when I was in school. These work sessions at home gave me quiet, focused time I could never find in the workplace—time to concentrate, think, and create. Doing my homework kept me on top of my workload and gave me the time to study important issues, read and digest critical documents, set strategies, and raise my level of expertise.

Make the Time

How do you find the time and discipline for homework once you leave school and start working 40-plus-hour weeks? Get rid of your television; then ditch all your friends! Seriously, a couple of hours of concentrated work at night can pay greater dividends than eight workday hours filled with interruptions and meetings. Yet you can't create this additional time—you can only allocate it. And you have to choose what is more important: your career or *Friends* reruns.

Log 40-Plus

It has been said that the first 40 hours you work each week are for your job, and every hour after that is for yourself. So true. I once read a *Fortune* magazine interview with the CEO of a billion-dollar company who declared his secret for success: "I keep up with my competition during the week—and pass them by on the weekends!" Logging extra hours on a consistent basis is one of the best-kept secrets among high achievers—it's how they leapfrog ahead of competitors, build distinguished careers, and ultimately make their mark.

Don't Overdo It

Please be clear: I'm *not* advocating workaholism, nor does homework have to be drudgery. If you have picked the right profession, and don't work yourself sick (which can certainly happen), working at home in the evenings can be an activity you'll anticipate and maybe even relish—but you must embrace it and ingrain it into your daily routine. Doing your homework faithfully is the best insurance policy I know of to guarantee that you keep learning, growing, and realizing your dreams.

Do Your Required Reading

Doing your homework mainly involves keeping up with your reading—which requires a segue from pedantic textbooks to trade journals, newsletters, company-specific material, and anything you think might give you an edge in your job. You may not have kept up in college, but you *must* in your career. Personally, my professional reading time was my number-one source of ideas and inspiration, and it gave me a quantum advantage. I can't emphasize this point enough. Reading exposes you to humankind's greatest insights and allows you to tap into other people's minds and experiences. Most importantly, it motivates you to take action and try things.

Give Your Boss a Scare

This means trying something that has never before been attempted; expanding the boundaries of your position far beyond your job description; and taking calculated, intelligent risks that just might make your boss decidedly anxious. Make no mistake: I'm not suggesting reckless, foolish risk taking; however, I am a proponent of pushing limits; venturing into the unknown; and making extreme, though well-conceived, gambles. If your initiatives pay off, you can expect more rewards, recognition, and respect—*yet possibly a boss who takes all the credit!*

Get Yourself Fired

I realize this is perhaps my most outlandish and controversial piece of advice. I recommend that rookie professionals break the rules or at least break the boss's composure, because it just may do for you what it did for me—get you fired. I was sacked three times in my career: at 22, by my first employer; at 24, by a major client; and at 38, by the multinational firm that bought my company. (The third time was the consummate charm seeing as the severance package was quite remarkable.) When I allude to getting fired, I don't mean for a white-collar crime like embezzlement or corporate espionage. I don't even propose actually getting terminated, although that may be the consequence. What I'm advocating is having the courage and conviction to "sin bravely," which I define as operating in someone else's best interest without his or her knowing it at the time. And what will happen if you go too far? You'll get your future freed up, and you'll have the chance to apply your skills somewhere else. That's what happened to me, and I've certainly survived to tell about it.

Don't Have Trepidation over Termination

At this point you might be wondering, "just exactly how will getting canned help my career?" Four ways: First, it will terrorize you, especially if you don't see it coming (which was the case when I got sacked the first time).

You'll run scared for a while, but the fear will serve as a catalyst for something better. Second, it will force you to take a careful inventory of what skills and special talents you possess for which somebody else might pay you even more. Third, it will motivate you to think bigger in terms of your true potential, and the degree to which you've been realizing it. Fourth, the process of recovering from it will give you a newfound independence, greater self-reliance, and a deeper understanding of human behavior—your own and others'. So don't fear getting fired—it may well do more good for your career than bad, and it'll season you like nothing else. If the day ever comes when you are relieved of your job responsibilities, don't panic. In fact, celebrate—it may ignite your career.

Don't Waste the Surplus Decade

As I said earlier, no matter what your age—and assuming you are healthy—you can still expect to reap the bonus decade. Whether you are in midlife or retirement, you can take advantage of these extra years. You can earn your college degree (or another one), recharge or change your career, start a business, pursue some new passion, make a whole new set of friends, and even get yourself axed from your job. Just because you may not have fully utilized your 20s doesn't mean you can't put the additional time to good use now and achieve the benefits you may have missed the first time around. Hey, an extra 10 years is an extra 10 years—*no matter when you capitalize on it.*

Have Some Fun, Too

All work and no play makes Jack and Jill duller than dirt, so there must be a balance between work and play. Know that you can work 50-hour weeks and still have a life. In fact, even if you sleep solid eight every night, you'll have another 60-plus hours per week for other pursuits. It's a smart idea to be conscientious about both work *and* play. So party on, Garth!

Behold Your Aspirations

Eleanor Roosevelt once said, "The future belongs to those who believe in the beauty of their dreams." I would add, "Dream young and dream old, for your dreams line the road to well-being and fulfillment." And if these words don't inspire you . . .

Listen to Steve Jobs

I want to leave you with an impassioned plea that Jobs made to me shortly after he was fired from Apple Computer, the legendary company he founded in his 20s. As you may know, it took Jobs nearly a decade to fully recover from being let go, but he eventually emerged as one of America's wealthiest billionaires with his animation company, Pixar, and the reemergence of Apple (thanks to the iPod's popularity). It was profound advice he imparted then, and I believe his words still resonate today with a whole new generation: "Follow your heart, but do it with your head."

Chapter TWO

Making Your Days Count

Days Add Up

Consider 86,400 seconds; 1,440 minutes; 24 hours. One day—it's the fundamental unit of time.

Surely you've noticed how some days fly by while others drag on. There are times you accomplish more in a day than in a week and times you can't recall completing a single thing during the day just ended. Certain days are a blast, and others, a wipeout.

Think about your sunrise-to-sunset. Do your mornings begin with excited anticipation and leap-out-of-bed enthusiasm? Do your evenings end with laughter and contentment? Or do you start your day with dread and finish it regretting you've failed to achieve (and enjoy it) more? Or worse, do you fall into bed at night relieved you've simply survived another date on the calendar?

What about the quality of your daily routines? Are they brimming with interesting challenges, fulfilling work, and rich experiences? Or would you characterize them as ho-hum, same-as-yesterday mundane, and, by and large, filled with meaningless tasks?

How do you organize your waking hours? Are you a creature of habit, dividing your time into orderly capsules, or do you prefer spontaneity and serendipity?

What undermines an ideal day? Distractions? Interruptions? Bad news? Certain difficult people? Travel?

Traffic? Insufficient or restless sleep? Too much crammed into too little? When your days "run away from you," what's going on?

And finally, what constitutes a day of distinction? How does a day stand out as productive, satisfying, and memorable? Conversely, what makes for one you'd like to forever forget?

Decisive answers to these questions will help define your model day so you'll waste fewer and relish more. Your days are finite and precious, and if you plan them wisely, they'll add up to a life of nominal regrets, considerable achievement, and supreme self-satisfaction.

A Day to Remember

Think about the special days in your life: your high school graduation, your wedding day, milestone birthdays, and the days your children were born. Most of us have collected memorable days like these, but what about those unexpected yet extraordinary ones? Do you recall living one in particular that stands out above the rest? I do—in June of 1974, shortly after I turned 17.

It started on a late Friday afternoon when I was hanging around with three of my closest buddies, Frank, John, and Louie. The school year had just ended, and Louie announced it was his birthday. Itching to celebrate and do something adventuresome before our summer jobs kicked in, we began tossing around ideas. We couldn't agree on anything until John blurted out, "Hey, what about driving up to Provincetown?" That's all it took to set our journey in motion.

Back then "P-town" was considered an ultra-happening place. A funky, laid-back beach town, it sits at the extreme tip of the Cape Cod peninsula, 50 miles southeast of Boston and about five hours from East Hartford, our hometown. Tourists flock there in the summertime, attracted to the artsy boutiques, lively bars, and bohemian restaurants, which flank the cobblestone walkway running through the main village. The peninsula is also famous for its pristine white beaches and mammoth sand dunes.

After quickly working out the details (like selling our parents on the idea and figuring out if we had enough money), we piled into John's Pontiac and took off. Halfway to Provincetown, we stopped in Newport, Rhode Island, and camped out in the basement of Frank's college roommate, Denny, who would join us the following day. At dawn, after almost no sleep, the five of us crammed into the car and finished the final leg of the trip, arriving in time to have breakfast at a local cafe.

It was a spectacular day, without the usual thick humidity and hazy sky characteristic of New England beaches. We spent the morning meandering through village shops, purchasing groovy necklaces and bracelets, and lazing on park benches to watch the people. After grabbing some hotdogs, we headed for the water. We did it all—bodysurfed, raced up and down the water's edge in our cutoffs, played volleyball, and built crooked sand castles—all the while making sure we didn't miss a single bikini.

Eventually succumbing to hunger pangs, we returned to the village and squeezed into a tiny fish joint Denny had heard about. We sat elbow to elbow with the noisy crowd, devouring platter after platter of mouthwatering steamed clams and crab legs. We stuffed ourselves silly.

With plenty of sunlight left, we wandered back to the beach—and then onto the sand dunes. As I recall, it was Louie who first took a running leap and flew off a dune. Following his lead, we sprinted and bounded off the dunes, soaring at least 20 feet before landing in the soft sand. Trying to outdo one another, we became increasingly more daring, attempting front flips, back flips, and 360s. Our gentle landings lowered our fear factor, while each daunting feat escalated our cockiness. After what seemed like hours, we found ourselves covered with sand from head to toe—it was lodged in our scalps, in our ears, under our nails. But the thrill of dune jumping more than compensated for the grittiness, and a quick dip in the Atlantic solved the problem, rejuvenating us at the same time.

We drifted back to the dunes and sprawled out under a lone pine tree perched at the highest point. It was nearly nine o'clock. No one said a word as we watched the red sun dissolve into the bluish-gray horizon. What a classic, magical moment: five close friends on the brink of adulthood, huddled together, celebrating the end of what, to us, was a flawless day. It was a magnificent time—no worries, no responsibilities—one carefree day to just *be*, a day I relished and will never forget.

Decades later I still reminisce about that special time. I remember everything—the sights, the smells, the sounds, the sea, and the sand dunes. But, mostly, I cherish the camaraderie we shared. In my lifetime, it was a day that really counted.

How about You?

When you reflect back on your memorable days, how many and which ones come to mind? What were you doing? With whom? Was it an activity or a conversation you remember? What insights and fine points can you recall? How do those days stand out in a substantive way? Go ahead . . . either in your head or on paper, try to record all of the days you truly remember. I bet you'll be stunned at how few you can summon up.

I contend that most people cannot recollect even 1 percent of their days on earth. It's especially difficult when most of our days are so easy to dismiss—routine days, when nothing out of the ordinary happened. For the vast majority, far too many of those are just a blur, with no remembrance of even having taken a breath. I call them "nothing days."

I would also argue that the memories we *do* collect are mostly good ones. Why? Because our minds naturally filter out most of the bad ones, sublimating awful experiences, bitter disappointments, and once-great relationships gone sour. Instead, we dwell on the gratifying times, retrospecting the good old days of our past. It's human nature to do this, I'd say.

Yet some folks do fixate on the painful memories of life. Those days are certainly significant as well, and they can also teach us valuable lessons, such as behaviors we'll not repeat and words we'll never speak again. But ultimately, making good memories is a matter of choice, and happens one day at a time.

Counting Your Days

One March morning in 1995, I was sitting at the desk in my study in a daze, contemplating some big decisions I had to make and how they might affect my life. I was staring blankly through my picture window at the Rocky Mountain range, unsure of what to do. For some reason, mathematics and mortality simultaneously popped into my head, breaking my trance.

I decided to calculate the number of days in an average lifetime. I've always been fascinated by statistics, so I did the math. It was simple: Multiply the average lifetime of 75 years (based on actuarial charts at that time) by 365 days, add 20 leap-year days, and you get 27,395 days in an average lifetime. For females it's about 1,100 more, and for males it's about 1,100 less.

Then my curiosity really kicked in, and I computed how many days I had lived and how many I had left if I were to live an average-length life. That's when it hit me—I had fewer days in front of me than behind me, and I was not quite 38! Wow . . . more of my life behind than in front of me. Married only a couple of years with an infant child, yet I had less than half of my life to live. It was an illuminating but still sobering thought.

Consider some statistics I've calculated for you, depending on your age. Table 2.1 begins at age 25, because prior to that, most young adults think they're going to live forever.

TABLE 2.1 Life Expectancy Chart

Age	*Months Left*	*Weeks Left*	*Days Left*	*Hours Left*
25	600	2,600	18,250	438,000
30	540	2,340	16,425	394,200
35	480	2,080	14,600	350,400
40	420	1,820	12,775	306,600
45	360	1,560	10,950	262,800
50	300	1,300	9,125	219,000
55	240	1,040	7,300	175,200
60	180	780	5,475	131,400
65	120	520	3,650	87,600
70	60	260	1,825	43,800

75 (Based on average life expectancy, you're on borrowed time from this point forth!)

Of course, you may actually have fewer days left than you think. The chart is just a guideline—certainly not a guaranteed minimum. Some people die prematurely and don't get their fair share of life to live. Even though it's a downer to think about, accidents, terminal illnesses, war, and murder cut lives short. That's why it's especially important to add value to every day.

If you're my age, 48 as of this writing, more than half of your expected life has already passed you by (64 percent, to be exact). My point is that the most precious unit in life is *this* day, and you've got a finite number of them left to live. Some people may still tell you that you have your whole life in front of you, but that's not exactly true. The truth is, you have only today in front of you—a truth that is new again every morning. I don't mean to be overly somber, but it's paramount that you acknowledge that your life is going by, day by day.

Why think in such bounded terms? Because you don't want to cheat yourself by using up your limited supply of days on inconsequential activities and wasted effort. In the final analysis, what you accomplish in life is the sum total of what you accomplish every single day. Accordingly, by maintaining a consciousness that you will strive to live the life you choose, you will be inclined to do more of the things that give you a deep sense of satisfaction, and spend more time with the people you really care about. Otherwise, what and who are you living for?

Keeping this number-of-days-left mind-set won't guarantee you happiness and fulfillment, but it will increase your odds of living the life you want. So, dear reader, I urge you to figure out exactly how many days you have left, and what actions you'll take—starting today—to add meaning to your life. After all, if you don't make your days count for something, you'll probably squander far too many of them and have serious regrets down the road. To avoid that unpalatable outcome, I offer the following merits of and modes for making your days matter.

Rewards of Making Your Hours Add Up

Feel in Control of Your Destiny

You're driving this bus called "your life." When you live it with purpose, passion, and pride, you determine the destination, how comfortable the ride is, and how far you travel. Regardless of the life stage you're in—young adult, rookie professional, seasoned professional, young parent, empty nester, or retired senior, you'll have a sense of confidence about the future and what it can hold. The timeworn line—*if you don't know where you're going, any road will take you there (or you might end up someplace else)*—may be a cliché, but it still rings true.

Something to Show for Your Days

It's gratifying when your days add up to something measurable, be it quantifiable career accomplishments or simply raising a healthy, happy child. Whether you're a scientist working toward a cure for a rare disease, a lawyer seeking to build a favorable record of cases, an artist creating a body of work, or a teacher attempting to enlighten young minds, progress you can see every day is what it's all about. If you are focusing on work (versus relaxation and enjoyment), tangible output is the name of the game.

Live a Life Worth Living

That is, live a challenging, exciting, and fun life. You can fritter away your finite days on mundane, rote activities or turn up the amplitude and achieve something consequential. If you go simply through the motions of living—not fully engaging your mind and your heart, not giving your all, not pressing for your best—you'll have more than a couple of second thoughts in your twilight years. Make every day count, and your one-and-only life will surely count for something.

No Regrets

Make each of your days mean something, and you'll have no desire to relive them. You'll look back with satisfaction and forward with anticipation. You won't be laden with misgivings over hollow years (or maybe decades) void of rich memories and noteworthy attainments. Instead, you'll feel good about every stage of your life—especially the one you're in.

Methods for Making Every Minute Meaningful

Have a Plan and Plan Ahead

What do you want to accomplish with your life? Most people take more time planning a long weekend vacation than they do the rest of their lives. I encourage you to map out your life as far into the future as you can—a year out isn't too far. When you're aware of your job, family, and social commitments well in advance, you can be cogitating on how you'll deal with what lies ahead. You up the chances you'll meet deadlines, fulfill obligations, and spend quality time with family and friends. So eschew the mañana mentality.

Design Your Day the Evening Before

List your objectives and rank them according to priority. Then, estimate the time you'll need to complete each one. And don't kid yourself—it's amazing how people consistently underestimate how long their tasks will take. If you overfill a day, your major accomplishment will be a massive sense of frustration. Planning ahead pays off in four important ways: (1) You're more objective and less likely to postpone the unpleasant (but high-payoff) tasks. (2) With a just-completed day fresh in your mind, you know where your projects stand, and priorities more naturally become apparent. (3) Because all the ends are tied up, you can complete your workday with a clear mind, fully prepared to meet the next day's challenges. (4) The following morning you'll hit the ground running, knowing exactly where to start.

Set Pithy and Attainable Goals

Volumes have been written on the process and value of goal setting, and most people buy into the concept. But do you actually *do it*? Have you set realistic, measurable goals spread out over daily, weekly, monthly, quarterly, and yearly time increments? Have you focused on the few objectives that will make a difference in the quality of your life—and written them down? If so, do you look them over regularly to monitor your progress and reassess your commitment level? Do you do periodic gut checks to make sure your goals were reasonable from the outset? Unreasonable goals (e.g., lose 10 pounds in one week) cause us nothing but frustration and distress. What you make of your life is your responsibility alone, and goal setting is a tried-and-true method to keep you on track. One exercise I do every New Year's Day is review my annual goals from the previous year and determine what I would like to accomplish in the ensuing year. I'm not always pleased with last year's results, but the process forces me to examine how I spent my time, what I really achieved, and what I want to accomplish this year. Typically, I set goals in the following areas: health (target weight); diet (daily nutrition); exercise (workouts per week); continuing education (books and seminars); investments (portfolio and estate planning); career (speaking, writing, and consulting); hobbies (number of skiing days); reading (specific books and periodicals); and family (kid time, vacations, and fun activities). Use these categories as a guide for creating your own.

Know Your Rhythms and Blues

Think of yourself at six o'clock in the morning. What animal comes to mind? An eager beaver or last night's roadkill? When do you hit your stride: early morning, midmorning, midafternoon, or midnight? Schedule routine tasks and appointments for your low-energy or "blue" periods, and critical assignments and meetings for when you're more alert. Work with your daily rhythms and you'll be not only more productive but better off emotionally.

Build in Concentration Blocks

To ensure you get to your high priorities, you must set aside a portion of your day to think, create, and plan—no interruptions, no phones, no visitors, no distractions. I suggest you try at least one of the following: make an appointment with yourself, schedule a quiet hour, work from home, or go to the workplace early—or stay late. In fact, there may be days when you feel you've made your only real accomplishment during your concentration time.

Find Out How You're Spending Your Days

You may be surprised. One way to evaluate how you're *really* passing your days is to keep a log. It is merely a diagnostic tool and need not be a permanent addition to your routine. Here's how it works: For a full week, write down in 15-minute increments everything you do throughout the day. Most people resist this exercise, thinking it will take more time than it saves. Not true! The cumulative time you spend will be less than five minutes a day, yet it can help save hours. A week's worth of time charts will uncover misplaced priorities, recurring time wasters, and patterns of low productivity. If you're like most people, you'll be horrified at what your journal reveals. But the truth will liberate you, allowing you to engineer a day that lets you hit your mark.

Subtract Before You Add

Many productive, yet overworked people instinctively accept additional responsibilities without first letting go of others. They are forever pushing the limits on how far they can stretch their daily 24-hour allotment. Unfortunately, getting more efficient can gain you only so much additional time. At some point, it becomes imperative to determine which duties and obligations you must escape in order to take on new and more challenging ambitions. The next time you decide to do more, ask yourself, "What can I delegate or stop doing altogether?"

Create Space in Your Life

As a corollary to the previous point, what, specifically, can you do to gain extra hours? Some worthy ideas: If possible, shorten your commute by taking a job closer to home (a bold move, but the time savings could be substantial); negotiate with your boss to work one day a week at home (if you can resist the TV and refrigerator, you can work interruption-free and often double your productivity); curtail or omit rituals that don't bring you as much value as you may think (do you gain all that much using up an hour a day reading the newspaper or watching the local news?); if your body can handle it, sleep less each night (set the alarm for an hour earlier and don't touch the snooze button!); pay others to run your errands (my local Yellow Pages lists no fewer than five premier concierge services that, for a reasonable fee, will wash and fuel your car, grocery shop, drop off/pick up clothes at the dry cleaner's, and handle many other odds and ends—check yours); text message instead of calling (most cell phones have this function, but BlackBerrys and Treos make it a no-brainer); and be less available to certain people who rob you of time you could put to a more satisfying use. Also, what everyday activities can you eliminate—or mitigate? Here are the obvious ones: watching TV (cut out the entertaining but mindless programs—are the trendy reality shows eating up your valuable evening hours?); talking on the phone (rely on caller ID or voice mail to screen unwanted callers on both your landline and cell phone); and hanging out online (do you really need to fritter away *any* time in chat rooms?). Surely one of these suggestions can open up extra minutes (or hours) each day.

Be Ruthless with Time Wasters

Considering the plethora of calls, appointments, e-mails, errands, and interruptions most of us face, it is entirely possible to have perfectly active days during which you accomplish absolutely nothing of consequence. Unfortunately, many succumb to this temptation. But don't let it happen to you. Get tough and be merciless. Develop a mind-set that judges every activity in terms of whether it brings you closer, however minutely, to your goals. This practice enables you to recognize which meetings to skip, which appointments to cancel or cut short, and which projects or errands to delegate. You'll know when to say no. Even better, people will tune in to your no-nonsense approach and learn to respect your time as much as you do.

Budget Introspective Time

We all need time just to think . . . to think through our opportunities, our options, and our opinions. When is your ideal think time? In the early morning, late at night, on a walk, during your commute, while you exercise, when your mind wanders in church, sitting in your favorite chair, when you're doing the dishes? Take a minute to consider where you do your deepest contemplation, and acknowledge how essential it is you make room for and protect that time.

Establish Rituals and Routines

This is classic advice I'm sure you've read elsewhere, but it bears repeating: Go to bed and rise at the same time each day; consume meals at consistent, preset hours; know your high-productivity periods and do your most creative and challenging work then; exercise daily (I find early morning is best); and work the same schedule each day. Maintaining these patterns will help you maximize your productivity because you'll move naturally and rhythmically from one activity to the next. Of course, there will be occasional emergencies and deadlines that knock you off track, but do your best to stick with your quotidian routines.

Learn Something

Nothing nourishes the mind more than a fresh insight, a deeper understanding of how something works, an interesting and useful fact, or a newly acquired skill. Erudition leads to wisdom, which in turn leads to higher self-esteem—a good thing, indeed. If you are always open and hungry for knowledge, your days will add up intellectually as well. From my daily book reading over the past year alone, I've learned about the astonishing rise and fall of both Churchill and Hitler, two of the most controversial and powerful political figures of the twentieth century; I now understand the sensitive issues surrounding health care, the number-one crisis facing our country; I have a better grasp of globalization and its transforming effects on the world economy; and I've become enlightened to the hunger crisis that gripped Russia under Stalin's regime between the world wars. Further, viewing PBS documentaries has given me insights into the lives of U.S. Presidents Lincoln, Eisenhower, and Johnson, as well as author, speaker, and humorist Mark Twain and genius-scientist Albert Einstein. However you seek information, do it every day. (For more thoughts on how to be a lifelong learner, see Chapter 6, "Nourishing Your Mind.")

Do Your Best

I don't mean to sound like a high school coach delivering a pep talk, but when you give your all to your pursuits, your self-satisfaction meter never points higher—win or lose. Even though cruise-control mode can be tempting at times, give your personal best day in, day out. It's this bone-deep, from-the-soul commitment to operating at your peak that will make each day matter more than it might have.

Get Back on Track

Most of us sink into ruts now and then, feeling as though we're on a treadmill going nowhere. It's human, it's normal, and it's to be expected. When you're in a rut, your days slide by without even registering—they're the indiscernible ones that you merely get through versus genuinely live. If this occurs (and inevitably it will), don't even consider giving in to the slump. Rather, do a mind and soul search for what has caused you to stagnate, redirect your energies, and take little steps to forge your way back to your optimum performance. Otherwise, too many of your scarce days won't stand for much.

Connect with Loved Ones

Hooking up once a day with your nearest and dearest is one good way to enrich your life. And making contact can be so easy: a sit-on-your-lap chat with a young child; an instant message exchange with a sibling; a quick call to Mom or Dad; an out-of-the-blue, drop-in visit to a grandparent; a longer-than-usual family dinner (where everyone stays seated and engaged long after the meal has been consumed); or a late-night pillow talk with your spouse or significant other. Daily bonding with those who mean the most to you will make your days feel more complete.

Calculate Kid Time

A good friend once told me he had only 312 weekends left before his last child went off to college. At first, it struck me as funny that he would actually take the time to determine precisely how many Saturdays and Sundays remained until he and his wife would become empty nesters. And then I considered how close he was to his children and how important it obviously was for him to spend every possible weekend with them before they left for college. I subsequently started a running tally of the weekends left before my own children grow up and move out (I update it monthly, too). As a result, I think twice about saying yes to social events on weekend nights and overdoing adults-only weekend getaways, making a concerted effort to spend time with my children.

Do Something for Someone Else

A small, kind gesture, in and of itself, can make a day worthwhile not just for you, but also for someone else. When you know you've made a contribution to another's well-being, you feel more valuable to the world—and you help others feel valued as well. When we give of ourselves, we give our self-regard a boost.

Laugh a Lot

What's a day worth without a good laugh? Even better, how about a doubled-over belly laugh that makes tears run down your cheeks? Remember the last time you had one of those? Yes, I realize bad stuff can happen. But even in the worst of circumstances you can look for something to at least chuckle over. (If regular prompts would help, subscribe to an Internet joke-of-the-day web site—a Google search will lead you to hundreds of options.) Laughter lightens dark moods, takes your mind off problems, and gives you an emotional release like no other. Simply put, days when you laugh a lot can be your best days.

Unwind in Your Own Special Way

I remember when I was regularly logging 80-hour weeks in the go-go years of building my company. Regardless of how many hours I worked, it seemed there was still more I could be doing. I often commented that I could fill 24 hours a day with my workload if I could just find a way to live without sleep. But I couldn't and I didn't. Despite my long work hours most days, I still managed to find time to relax and have fun. Whether it was a good book, a first-run movie, favorite TV show, dinner with friends, or a day on the ski slopes, I would carve out time to get away from it all and recharge my batteries. I know these activities increased my productivity when I had to be *on*. They also provided some degree of life balance to the whirlwind schedule I maintained, making my days even more fulfilling.

Checklist Your Perfect Day

A tangible record of your days can be especially useful in changing how you live them. Put pen to paper and create a list of activities and impressions that identify your most memorable days. Each morning scan the list for a clear picture of a perfect-day prescription, and at bedtime glance at it again to determine how closely you adhered to it. Of course, you'll seldom be able to check off every item, but your brief review will certainly increase your odds of having good days. And if you are consistently checking too few items, the list will help you put your priorities back on track. Here's a sampling of what your checklist might include:

__Slept soundly
__Watched the sun rise and set
__Exercised
__Ate healthily
__Accomplished my top priority
__Completed a project
__Smiled and laughed
__Learned something
__Celebrated a success
__Fixed something
__Joked with kids
__Played a game
__Listened to music
__Danced
__Interacted with interesting people
__Called a relative
__Talked with a friend
__Responded to calls and e-mails
__Helped someone
__Resolved a conflict
__Volunteered
__Spent time outdoors
__Read a good book
__Watched an old movie
__Enjoyed a hobby
__Sat quietly
__Spent time alone
__Frolicked with significant other

Count Them All

Alternatively, you can add up your activities every day to help monitor how you are utilizing your time. I recommend measuring what's important to you in various categories—namely, career, family, recreation, hobbies, spiritual quests, volunteer work, or whatever will create the foundation for a significant day (use your checklist as a guide). And certainly don't force yourself to do activities just to enumerate them; instead, count them as a gut check to ensure you're including what you deem as mission-critical to your life's happiness and fulfillment.

Mark the Noteworthy Days in Some Way

Develop a consciousness for how you will remember the especially momentous days of your life by a word, picture, or sound association (whatever means works best for you). File these days in the attic of your mind under "treasured remembrances." Or you could be more pragmatic by marking your paper calendar in a unique way or inserting a seldom-used symbol on your personal digital assistant page (a search of the symbol will instantly display all entries). I grant you, not all days will be indelible or date-stamp worthy. In fact, many will be mundane and probably not the ones you'll reflect on down the road. Yet they can still be good days (that is, ones that count). The great ones, however, you never want to forget. And to that end . . .

Celebrate the Significant Ones

When was the last time you celebrated a big day? I'm not referring to the obligatory milestones such as a child's baptism or bar/bat mitzvah, your 40th birthday, or a 10th or 25th wedding anniversary, but rather to those occasions when you land a hard-earned promotion, receive a healthy report from your doctor, achieve a personal best in an athletic endeavor, or witness the special accomplishment of a child. Make the time to commemorate those landmarks in special ways with family and friends. However you choose to honor your historic events, try to do it more often. Don't forget—you are creating the good old days of some future time.

Overcome Procrastination

This point deserves its own chapter. It's next.

Chapter THREE

Triumphing over Procrastination

Getting off Dead Center

There is a simple reason why many of us never accomplish what we could—we just can't seem to get started.

Everyone procrastinates. Some people may be attempting to escape unpleasant or seemingly overwhelming tasks, while others are avoiding the prospect of failure. Still others may be hesitant to take risks or try something new, fearing change or confrontation. Whatever the origin, the consequences of putting it off can range from unease and frustration to severe anxiety and regret, and from mediocre work or missed deadlines to a catastrophic illness or financial devastation.

The key to overcoming this troublesome habit is recognizing that procrastination is generally "all in your head," a problem more of perception than reality. After all, dreading work is usually more agonizing than actually doing it.

In fact, soon after beginning a project, most people typically experience a burst of energy. Those of you who are distance runners, for instance, understand that the first mile is always harder than the second. Pushing past the initial barrier is what vanquishing procrastination is all about, because that's when you're warmed up, you've found your rhythm, and you're operating at peak efficiency. This is the state where working—like running—becomes a pleasure.

The by-product of conquering habitual procrastination, in addition to accomplishing much, much more, is the satisfaction of knowing that you have entered—and can enter at will—a place of hyperproductivity. All the elaborate excuses and avoidance games have disappeared. You're no longer facing that disquieting "night before it's due" feeling, *and* you're not missing deadlines. You're on top of things—where you belong. Don't let unrealistic fears prevent you from achieving what you're capable of. Consider Pablo Picasso's sage words, "Only put off until tomorrow what you are willing to die having left undone."

What's on Your "Still Haven't Gotten to" List?

Here are what I consider the top 20 most common procrastination pitfalls (along with some pointed queries):

1. *Writing your will*—For that matter, have you done *any* estate planning?
2. *Preparing a tax return*—How about, at a bare minimum, pulling together last year's statements and forwarding them to your accountant?
3. *Rebalancing your investment portfolio*—Is it time to meet with your financial adviser—or *find* one?
4. *Resolving a feud*—Just how long *can* you hold a grudge?

5. *Going for a promotion*—If you've been stalling on this one, what is it costing you career- and incomewise?
6. *Updating your resume*—When done properly, it should take two to three hours—what are you waiting for?
7. *Looking for a better job*—Have you checked out the postings on Monster.com lately?
8. *Doing homework*—Do you have any kids who always leave it until the last minute? (Perhaps like you did?)
9. *Packing for a trip*—Do you shelve it until 10 o'clock the night before?
10. *Making repairs*—How much water has been wasted by that dripping faucet?
11. *Resolving computer issues*—Can't get a program to function properly, so you're just living without it?
12. *Getting a physical exam*—Has it been more than a few years since your last "annual" checkup?
13. *Organizing the garage*—Can you even fit your car in there anymore?
14. *Cleaning carpets*—Do you keep moving the furniture to cover up the stains?
15. *Working out*—How many years have you been swearing to start and then stick with a regular routine?
16. *Going to the dentist*—What bothers you more: the pain you have now or the pain you might have in the chair? (Come on, with just a shot—or two—of Novocaine, you won't feel a thing.)

17. *Paying bills*—Does it take the threat of having your utilities turned off to motivate you to pull out your checkbook?
18. *Preparing a performance assessment*—Managers: How many weeks (months?) overdue are you on completing (starting?) Sally Smith's review?
19. *Writing a business plan*—It's hard to launch a business without one—how about writing the executive summary for starters?
20. *Getting your car serviced*—Do you subscribe to the change-the-oil-only-when-it-won't-start philosophy?

Guilty of a few? I certainly am. Is procrastination a more prevalent issue in your life than you are willing to concede? Ever thought long and hard about why you do it—and what it has cost you? (Or have you put that off, too?)

Why Do We Do It?

Fear lies at the root of procrastination—fear that a task will take longer, require more effort, or be filled with more daunting obstacles than you had envisioned. The most debilitating factor, however, is that you won't be able to do it—or do it well (translation: an overwhelming fear of flat-out failure). Intrinsically, most procrastinators doubt they can actually achieve what they have implied or said they could do—to themselves and others (something few may have the courage to admit).

I experienced this firsthand when I began writing this book. My original intention had been far more modest—merely to write a short essay and submit it to a men's magazine, such as *Esquire* or *GQ*. Although I had given considerable thought to both my topic and message, it took me a solid six months before I put pen to paper (or, in my case, fingers to the keyboard). I had managed to fall into the trap many writers succumb to: They hate *having* to write but love *having* written. A completed article ready for submission was incredibly appealing, but my enthusiasm stalled when it came to actually sitting down and recording my ideas. In truth, the fear that maybe I didn't have as much to say as I thought I did—or couldn't express myself creatively enough—triggered the procrastination impulse within me.

Once I overcame my fear and ultimately finished the piece, I hired a former employee to proofread my work (I hadn't published anything in several years and figured a once-over by a professional couldn't hurt). What I received back shocked me. She had crossed out entire sections, rewritten paragraphs, and jam-packed the margins with comments challenging much of my thinking—I saw more red ink from her pen than black ink from my printer. What horrified me more, however, was I agreed with the vast majority of her changes. Despite being a previously published author of two books, dozens of articles, and hundreds of marketing brochures,

I had to acknowledge that my composition wasn't nearly as polished as I had assumed. In fact, my writing left a lot to be desired.

Though valid, her edits were so extensive that when I attempted to integrate them, I felt overwhelmed and frustrated. Worse, the red-ink bloodbath I had to face confirmed my latent fear that perhaps I wasn't up for this challenge after all. So what did I do? Like a good procrastinator, I told myself I'd get to it later and filed it away—for about a year. Throughout that time, I convinced myself that other, more important projects demanded my attention, relegating the article to a much lower priority. Because I had set no firm deadline, I conveniently adopted the mind-set, "What's the rush?" I even stopped talking about my writing to family and friends, but inwardly I was disturbed by having not finished what I had started.

Eventually, I acknowledged that my writing skills had become rusty and the piece needed a major rewrite. As soon as I accepted this ego-bruising truth, I was able to incorporate the proofreader's suggestions, improving the article substantially. Ironically, I felt so pleased with the final product that I then envisioned it more as a chapter than as a magazine article and was inspired to write an additional seven chapters—which ultimately evolved into this book. I now regret not having come to terms with my angst much sooner.

When you can't seem to "get to it," as was my case, you rob yourself of the sheer joy of accomplishment, cheating yourself of the concomitant boost to your pride. Once you get moving and immerse yourself in a challenging assignment, you inevitably think, "Why did I wait? What a shame to have let so many days pass by."

Chronic procrastinators not only accomplish less than superconscientious overachievers, but also consciously or subconsciously postpone living life to its fullest—which is much more distressing. When you are prone to putting off what you deem important, your already limited number of days slides by, leaving you with less to show for them than you could have otherwise. The ugly, no-escaping-it truth is you're really wasting your life.

What Price Procrastination?

Dragging your feet can carry a hefty price tag—mentally, financially, and physically. First, consider the psychological costs in terms of perpetual anxiety, preoccupation with tasks left undone, and the consequent drop in self-esteem. "Not getting to it" becomes an albatross around your neck, refusing to release its grip. Indeed, procrastination has the opposite emotional impact of progress. Can you think of a time when this wasn't true for you?

Now, contemplate the practical penalties: Delay repairing a leaky roof and you risk ruinous interior damage to your home. Postpone maintaining your car and deterioration may be such that purchasing a new one becomes your only option. Pay your bills late and you could destroy your credit rating (not to mention having creditors hound you).

Lastly, ponder the implicit dangers of neglecting

your health. If you choose to ignore symptoms and/or avoid checkups, you could conceivably find yourself facing a debilitating illness, or at the extreme, death. To wit, a friend of mine put off seeing a doctor for several years about a growth on his back. The mole wasn't painful and he couldn't see it, making it all the more tempting to pretend the oddly formed pigmentation didn't exist. Eventually, though, the spot morphed into melanoma, infecting his body with tumors and forcing him into treatments that not only weakened his body further, but also failed to cure him. The fast-spreading cancer tragically took his relatively young life within a few years. Had he received medical attention even six months sooner, he might still be alive today. My friend paid the ultimate price for his procrastination. (Irony of all ironies, he sold life insurance for a living.)

Where Do You Fall in the Procrastination Continuum?

It's my contention that everyone puts something off to *some* extent. The critical question is, when do we stop dragging our feet and start taking action?

Consider a major work- or home-related project with a three-month time line. Highly motivated eager beavers generally take the first step within a few days after the deadline has been established. Moderate procrastinators may wait a couple of weeks before beginning and then make some degree of progress. Serious procrastinators often delay up to two months before even starting to think about the mission—or the looming cutoff date. Catastrophic postponers don't allow the task at hand to cloud their minds until the fated week prior. "Last-minute Larrys," the worst offenders, can't face what must be done until the dreaded night before. Maybe it's the adrenaline rush that fires them up to pull the inevitable all-nighter.

Where do *you* fall within this range? If you're a conscientious type who prefers to get an early jump, bravo. Chances are you live with less stress, seldom miss a deadline, and do consistently good work. If you're somewhere in the middle, you undoubtedly know the pressure of wishing you had started earlier, and you turn in work that's occasionally subpar. If you're a candidate for Procrastinators Anonymous, I'm betting you live on caffeine, thrive on nervous energy, and seldom deliver your best. Regardless of your disposition, here are the advantages of making your move promptly, followed by techniques that will help you find the self-discipline to tackle without delay—and with enthusiasm—even the most loathsome of projects.

Payoffs of Not Putting It Off

You'll Win More Than You Lose

As my high school football coach used to say every day in practice, the team that "gets off the line" quicker will generally control the line of scrimmage—and win the game. The same can be said for track-and-field sprinters:

Most races are won in the starting blocks. If you start with a surge, expect that you'll experience more victories than you will defeats.

Par Excellence

We kid ourselves when we think we need deadline pressure to deliver our finest effort. Occasionally we luck out and score a two-minute-drill touchdown, but more often than not, we simply "run out of clock" and lose the game. Give yourself the time to do it right, and your performance will noticeably improve.

Less Angst

Is there anything more stressful than having a critical project haunting your brain with nonstop reminders of a threatening deadline—and you've done little or nothing toward seeing it through? Depending on how long you have been procrastinating, the awareness that you've taken minimal or no action can lead to panic attacks. Sheer terror may ensue as each day passes and the deadline closes in. You may begin to wonder nervously how to make up for lost time or start worrying about the serious consequences of being late, beating yourself up for having delayed in the first place. When you dive in immediately and make perceptible headway, these negative thoughts rarely invade your psyche. Moreover, you have one less thing weighing on your conscience, freeing up mental space for other issues vying for attention. Unfettered by drama and paralyzing dread, your productivity rises while your blood pressure falls. Why not choose action and experience the positive emotional effects?

Enjoy the Ride

When you're always under the gun dealing with life's details, your pulse races, making it virtually impossible to find pleasure in the journey. When you are excruciatingly behind schedule, you may dissolve into a stressed-out mess, causing those around you to become alarmed and anxious. By guaranteeing enough runway to ensure a smooth takeoff, you will find that your contentment will increase in conjunction with your output.

Heightened Self-Respect

It's not only a matter of fulfilling your duties, but also a matter of pride. Believing in yourself becomes difficult when you leave everything to the last minute, never allotting adequate time to perform at your peak. "Putting it off and putting it out of your mind" can cause your self-worth to slip a few notches, whereas "getting to it and getting it done" can make you feel good about yourself. Let's face it: Persistent procrastination is a less than admirable character trait that thwarts us in more ways than we care to enumerate. And what about the price you pay in terms of respect from others? (See the next point.)

A Dependable Reputation

Don't allow your position among peers to suffer as a consequence of such a common problem as this enormous time, energy, and morale waster. Others know who stays on top of work assignments and who doesn't. Gaining and maintaining the esteem of colleagues is far easier when you are recognized as someone who gets the job done—consistently and expediently. Avoid leaving hot pots on the back burner!

A Better Way to Live

Always being behind the eight ball is a shoddy way to go through life. You can view time discipline, then, as the dual process of "de-horrible-izing" tasks and inviting achievement. Imagine yourself drifting along making zero progress on your goals versus charging ahead, energized, knocking off one goal after the next. You have a choice: Either you can expend mental energy on the "not doing" of the task or you can devote constructive energy in the doing of it, feeling galvanized in the end. Switching from a mind-set of "I'll get to it tomorrow" to "I'll do it today" is a tough transition. But it's worth it.

Fail-Safe Techniques for Diving In

Be Certain You Can Do It

Before taking on a job, make sure you have what's essential to accomplish it. A neighbor of mine had been putting off fixing a broken chair for months when he finally admitted he had neither the tools nor the expertise—nor the interest, for that matter—to accomplish it. He decided that calling a furniture repair expert was the best approach. The chair was as good as new within a week—after he had sat on it (!) for half a year. Being realistic about your skills and motivation can go a long way toward helping you achieve your goals.

Plot It Out

Once you commit to a project, map out the entire job—in writing. That will make it clearer, more tangible, and *doable*. If you start an endeavor that lacks focus, you'll invariably perceive it as being more complicated than it might otherwise be, opening the door to procrastination. By illustration, let's say you decide to paint your living room, which may seem daunting to some. Begin by thinking it through and then putting those thoughts on paper. Make a list of simple steps similar to these:

1. Determine the amount of paint required (measure the square footage of the surfaces you intend to paint).
2. Make a list of supplies you'll need (i.e., paint, brushes, rollers, paint trays, masking tape, edger, and drop cloths).
3. Take carpet and fabric samples from home to the paint store and select a color scheme.
4. Purchase supplies.

5. Move or cover the furniture, then take down wall hangings.
6. Cover the floor with drop cloths.
7. Mask off areas *not* to be painted.
8. Paint the ceiling.
9. Clean the brushes, rollers, and paint trays.
10. Paint the walls.
11. Inspect your paint job and do minor touch-ups.
12. Clean the brushes, rollers, and paint trays—again.
13. Remove covers and cloths, and replace the furniture.
14. Wash the painter!

When you take the time to plot out a task, you'll learn precisely what is entailed, helping you to avoid the pitfall of either under- or overestimating the process. Additionally, you may realize ways to delegate tasks. And following an orderly list not only will focus the project, but as you complete each step and cross it off, you'll also see the end approaching, motivating you toward the finish line.

Create a File

This is the easiest method for getting off the dime, *and* you can do it in under a minute. When you set up a file (computer or paper), the dreaded undertaking, suddenly less intimidating, is now officially under way. Having a place to store anything relevant to the job at hand can provide a sense of organization and, thus, act as a catalyst, triggering you to tackle the next steps in the process.

Once a file exists, it's amazing how quickly you start filling it with material required for the project. When you can't bring yourself to even think about an unwieldy assignment, reach for a fresh file and label it.

Break It Up

Anything is less disheartening when broken into pieces. If you have an intricate project looming (a major product launch, for example), don't just say to yourself, "I've got to get that project done." Instead, tell yourself, "This morning, I'm *just* going to outline the product features and benefits for our promotional brochure copy," making the task far more manageable. You'll find that completing the project in this step-by-step manner will prove easier than you initially thought possible, with the additional benefit that you feel much more relaxed in the process.

Do Something Now

Simply begin somewhere, anywhere. Don't stop to think—just take a deep breath, hold your nose, and jump. And do it as soon as you feel the slightest inspiration. For instance, as soon as painting the living room pops into your head, gather your fabric samples right away—certainly before the day is over. Now the momentum is with you. Have to file your tax return in two weeks? Don't dwell on the dread. Start pulling together all necessary documents, including receipts and 1099s. Taking action feels good, doesn't it? Watch out, though. If it feels *too* good, you may get smug and think the project is under control, a terrific excuse for further procrastination. The solution: read on.

Do It for 10 Minutes

However minuscule, make some progress on that assignment you've been avoiding. After 10 wholehearted minutes (come on, you can do just about *anything* for 10 minutes), reconsider. If you choose to quit, go ahead and quit. Chances are, though, you'll realize the job isn't nearly as horrendous as you had anticipated, and you'll be propelled into continuing. So get hold of a timer and set it.

Remind Yourself How Good You Are

Suppose you're a middle manager and must reprimand one of your employees—a thorny responsibility. Don't lose track of the fact that you have to do this *because* you've risen to management—and your ability to interact well with others is one of the key reasons you earned that position. Undoubtedly, you are adept at criticizing people in a positive way. So, remember this, especially when you're braving the demanding parts of your job—the things you're most tempted to postpone—since you need all the self-assurance you can marshal.

Deal with the Worst First

I recommend beginning your day with your most disagreeable chore. Have to mend fences with an angry customer? Pick up the phone the second you sit down at your desk. By doing so, you'll demonstrate to yourself that, yes, you *are* capable of undertaking the most distasteful issues right off the bat, making the remainder of your daily responsibilities that much easier to face. The ultimate goal is to change your mode of thinking from "This is unpleasant; I don't want to do it" to "This is unpleasant; I'd better do it now and get it over with." You can develop a momentum that feeds off itself. When the worst is over, you can expect smoother sailing as the day continues. Finish your vegetables before indulging in dessert!

See It as All Done

It has been said that people procrastinate when they cannot anticipate achievement. The following exercise helps you bust through that barrier by vividly showing you what achievement feels like. Close your eyes and relax. . . . Imagine you have just successfully accomplished your project and are basking in the glow of having realized another goal. Visualize every aspect of the process: the niggling details, the hang-ups, the breakthroughs. Concentrate particularly on the elation of completion. This simple exercise makes any endeavor seem less formidable. Where you once felt dread, you may now feel a flicker of exhilaration.

Shout It from the Rooftops

Committing yourself publicly to something can be a negative motivator, in that your goal becomes not to gain a reward but to avoid embarrassment. On the other hand, it *can* be effective. Case in point: You have been putting off calling a promising but particularly hard-to-score sales prospect. Announce to your boss and coworkers you intend to land the account or, at minimum, make a presentation to a decision maker. Then, invite them to monitor your progress weekly. Their watchful eyes will spur you onward.

Bribe Yourself

The next time you have a particularly laborious chore to perform, promise yourself a reward for getting it done by a certain deadline. This helps fixate your attention on the objective while making its accomplishment even more appealing. The incentive could be dinner out, a day off, or concert tickets—anything that will motivate you sufficiently. Be mindful, though, not to cheat by rewarding yourself prematurely (despite your newfound acceptance of self-bribery, you must maintain *some* pride). Cheating not only would deprive you of the chance to compensate yourself guilt-free, it would further serve to reinforce your dawdling.

Conduct a Self-Brainstorm Session

The yet-to-be-started, due-in-less-than-a-week assignment is now plaguing your every thought. You have known about it for months, yet you haven't a clue where to begin and "ain't done a thing." Try this. Take yourself out for coffee with a laptop (or writing pad) as your date. With your jolt of java within reach, open to a blank page and let the what-I-must-do thoughts flow. Make a bulleted list of how to attain each of your objectives; don't worry about prioritizing—simply fill the pages with ideas. This exercise can energize you either by helping you see there's not as much to the project as you originally foresaw or by terrorizing you with all that must be done in the next few days. Either way, you'll be hypermotivated to get moving. (Incidentally, fear can be an excellent motivator when serious consequences are involved.)

Become an Automaton

This dehumanizing technique just may work like a charm when all else has failed. Automatons don't concern themselves with losing face, they have no concept of self-confidence, and they don't respond to rewards. All they know is "Do it." That's how my colleague Robert describes his morning running routine: "When the alarm rings at 5:30 A.M., I don't think about how warm it is in my bed and how cold it is outside. I don't think about maintaining my health or living longer. I don't even think about how good I'm going to feel when I'm done. I don't allow *anything* to enter my mind. I simply reach out and turn off the alarm, get up, throw on my running gear, and put one foot in front of the other."

Do Something Else Instead

Sometimes you just can't muster the moxie to embark on a job. You may have everything you need, but you're not mentally prepared to dive in. Fine. Go after another overdue, but less onerous activity—organize a closet, clean out old files, return a phone call, or run an errand. As long as you're dealing with some issue you've allowed to slide, you can feel uplifted by finally trimming your list of neglected tasks. Sidestepping in this manner can actually clear your mind, providing you the impetus to address more weighty projects.

Overcome Inertia

I have a plaque that has sat on my desk for decades. It reads:

> *Two Steps to Success . . .*
>
> 1. *Get Started!*
> 2. *Don't Quit!*

Shift Your Self-Image

If you have always considered yourself a procrastinator, now is the time to envision yourself as a get-up-and-go, make-it-happen type. Look to the next chapter, which deals with taking initiative, to coach you in how to do this.

Chapter FOUR

Making Things Happen

The Antidote to Procrastination

He's a mover and a shaker. She's a can-do woman. They're taking the world by storm. We hear these catchphrases every day. They reflect our society's fascination with and respect for achievement. But how does achievement happen, and what separates self-starters from the multitudes stuck spinning their wheels?

Those who succeed personally and professionally know how to take charge. Self-confident and unafraid to take risks, they ferret out and exercise opportunities, setting plans in motion. They continually search for innovative approaches to impact their environment, having learned how to view the world in a manner that spawns not only major breakthroughs but a steady stream of small gains as well. Achievers have a knack for solving old problems in new ways.

Whereas the previous chapter addressed getting off dead center, getting to it, and getting it done, this chapter focuses on sparking initiation—creating the flight plan, seizing the controls, barreling down the runway, and taking flight.

Academia versus Real Life

It's no small wonder that many of us are mired in self-doubt and indecisiveness. For more than 150 years, schools have done little to promote and reward initiative; rather, they have discouraged—and even punished—independent thought and action. Our current educational system arose from the demands of the industrial revolution, a period when society was markedly different than it is now. The original academic approach, which remains essentially unchanged today, was based on rote learning, associating achievement with how well and how quickly students regurgitated the presented material.

Recall your own 12 to 16-plus years in school. Typically, a teacher handed out a writing assignment, and laid out precisely what to do ("eight pages, typed, double-spaced") and where to find the necessary information. You wrote the paper, handed it in, and got your grade. Then you waited for the next assignment. Raised and trained in such an environment, the vast majority of us are ill prepared to take the lead, finding it difficult to make any significant move on our own.

Strangely enough, outside of academia our society delivers quite the opposite message by rewarding innovation and celebrating the pioneering spirit. Accordingly, to prosper in the real world, you must step back from your scholastic roots and adopt a new protocol:

First, you must actually give yourself assignments,

although you may seldom know exactly what to do. If you think about your situation both at home and at work, you can probably name a hundred things you *could* do to be more effective, but which one(s) *should* you choose? (In truth, how often have you thought, "If someone would just tell me what to do, I'd do it"?)

Second, you may have to regularly make decisions and take action based on insufficient information, frequently without having any guaranteed outcome. Paradoxically, we're living in the information age—we're drowning in information—and yet we still may not have exactly what we need (or we may feel overwhelmed by its profusion). Either way, to be an accomplished initiator, you must occasionally rely solely on your instincts for guidance.

Finally, establishing deadlines becomes your responsibility, a challenging task because something can always be done to a higher standard with just a little more time. Adding to the entire mix is the possibility you won't know how well you've done for weeks or months, or even years.

Rocketing ahead in the real world, therefore, entails unlearning the safe, wait-to-be-told posture of your childhood and acquiring the skills necessary to tap into your creativity, formulate ideas, and then put those ideas into play. And, as with overcoming procrastination, you must avoid allowing the fear of failure, or of making a mistake, to thwart adopting this assertive philosophy.

You *can* become a champion initiator in every aspect of your life, whether it's in devising a plan for overhauling your personal finances, organizing a fund-raiser for your local schools, proposing a ballot initiative to improve your town, or developing a new product and starting your own business. When you resolve to set your life in motion, you become a player instead of a spectator. And though being the driver certainly has its material rewards, the good feeling of accomplishment and control over your life is even better.

I Can Do That . . .

Early in my career, I learned a powerful lesson about grabbing the bull by the horns. Nearly three decades ago, in the initial month of my first job, my boss asked that I take on the role of accounts receivable clerk. Since the company was small and everyone already wore many hats, this least-coveted responsibility fell to me—the low man on the totem pole. I'll never forget the thick file of unpaid invoices unceremoniously dropped on my desk. Given neither guidance nor background knowledge of the accounts, my directive was to collect more than $20,000 of billings that were, in some cases, six months past due. Compounding the problem were the many governmental clients (ever tried collecting money from the U.S. government?), some of whom had not been impressed (or were, at best, minimally satisfied) with the service they had received.

Despite zero experience, I dove with relish into these delinquent and seriously questionable receivables.

I began by preparing a simple hand-drawn spreadsheet using a ruler and pencil (desktop computers had yet to be invented), and listing the accounts and contact information. Then, starting at the top of the list, I called each creditor's accounts payable department, but was frequently transferred to other divisions. Unaware of any alternative procedure, I persisted, becoming "the little collector engine that could," until ultimately payment was authorized. Ironically and unbeknownst to me, many of these receivables were about to be written off.

Within one month, I had collected 90 percent of the monies due my company. Inevitably, this caught the company president's attention and, in the process, earned me the privilege of advancing to more challenging and lucrative projects. No one was more surprised than I with the appreciation and respect this effort brought me.

When I reflect back on the notable successes of my life, it's clear that many occurred because, at the time, I didn't fully understand what I was getting myself into. More naive than undaunted, I plunged into projects for which I lacked any meaningful know-how, seldom having a clue I might be in over my head. I simply plowed forward and figured out what I needed as I went along, relying primarily on common sense and stick-to-itiveness. Undeterred by fear (heck, I generally didn't even know enough to *be* afraid), I took chances and was never tempted to drag my feet when there was a conception that looked promising.

The following sections spotlight the most compelling

arguments for adopting the mind-set of a die-hard initiator and surefire ways to get things kicked off.

Top Reasons to Take Charge

Self-Empowerment

When you regularly go out on a limb and launch ideas, you can build an inner conviction that will serve you well in all aspects of your life. Your heightened self-confidence will breed a certainty that you will be able to solve most, if not all, problems, and that you can and *will* get it done—on time, on budget, on plan.

Be Viewed as a Go-To Person

It's gratifying to earn a reputation as an authentic go-getter. Think of the classic saying, "If you want something done, give it to a busy person." You can *be* that person. And when others see you as consistently making the first move and putting plans in motion, you will find yourself among the upper echelon of achievers in any group.

Claim the Choice Assignments

Once you demonstrate the courage to conquer the unknown, the energy to pursue opportunities, and an unwavering, let-me-at-it disposition, you will often be invited to cherry-pick the coveted jobs. Because you've repeatedly proven your zealousness in going after a desired outcome, those consigning the work won't hesitate in allowing you to select the projects (and teams) you most want to join.

Sense of Sovereignty

If you distinguish yourself as someone who can "run with it," employers tend to leave you alone. They trust your instincts and rely on your sound judgment, affording you the authority and resources to do things your way. Being granted such liberty and leeway is a definite plus, careerwise. Wouldn't you prefer this independence to a breathing-down-your-neck boss?

Become an A-Player Magnet

An initiator's infectious energy attracts friends and colleagues alike. If you establish yourself as someone who can catapult hot projects and see them through, other star performers will gravitate toward your team and want to work on your behalf. This attribute will only mushroom as talent flows your way, making for and sustaining a promising career. Further, you're likely to benefit in volunteer situations when you need to rely on friends, acquaintances, and neighbors to accomplish objectives in your community.

Move to the Front of the Class

Pioneering behavior can expedite your ascent in the world. It's the difference between being *in* the pack and *leading* the pack. You become the one who seizes the moment, commands the charge, and sets the pace. Throughout my 20 years' experience of overseeing 2,500-plus employees, it was, unfailingly, the initiators who rose through the ranks of the organization, regardless of the track they chose (i.e., management or specialist).

Reap the Rewards

There's something to be said for those who have a pattern of taking initiative and seeing things to completion—and it's usually said in terms of raises, bonuses, stock options, perks, and general accolades. If you foster a make-it-happen attitude, others will regard you as deserving of additional remuneration for the extra effort you invest. When it comes to sharing the spoils, go-getters get a bigger piece of cake.

Be a Model

With a knack for kicking things off, you can stand as a beacon for others, inspiring protégés, coworkers, and children to emulate you. Your proactive outlook will infuse any environment with optimism.

Innovative Concepts for Igniting Initiation

Commandeer the Undesirable

Many of the best opportunities for initiative lie in projects nobody wants. So sign up. Others will gladly step aside while you take the lead, affording you the autonomy to transform the project into a career milestone. A few years ago, an acquaintance of mine, Linda, had just started working in a retail store and volunteered to take inventory. Naturally, because it was a considerable undertaking—and one of the most dreaded in retail—no one was angling for it. Her supervisor jumped at the offer, saying, "What the heck—give it a shot." Linda accepted the challenge, produced thorough reports, and soon became the resident expert on inventory and its control procedures. Colleagues came to her with questions, respected her opinions, and followed her recommendations. As often happens in life, building credibility in one area leads to credibility in many. Linda is now running the shop.

Convert What You've Already Created

Think about your previous work. Can it be transformed into something else, thereby leveraging past efforts? Can the memos you've written your staff be turned into a policy manual? Can the market research you've done on one area of your business be applied to another? Consider a project you undertook but stalled on because you had neither sufficient information nor the proper tools to complete it—are there elements worth salvaging? Never let good work go to waste. Resurrect it. Find a new application. Recycling is one of the most powerful achievement principles available to you.

Search for Trouble

Adopt the highly effective practice of asking yourself throughout the day, "What's going on here?" Step outside yourself and assess what you are doing; what your employees are doing (if you're in management); even what your boss, competitors, suppliers, and customers are doing. What's not working? What could be improved upon? When you open your eyes—and actively seek trouble spots—you'll notice possibilities for initiative everywhere. The trick is to *do it.* You must lift your nose from the grindstone long enough to size up your situation. Until this becomes second nature, consider using a digital watch and setting it to buzz every couple of hours as a reminder. You'll be surprised at just how enlightening this technique can be.

Teach Thyself

This motto is crucial for the initiator. Anytime you see a way to make yourself more valuable to your organization, beyond your current duties, pursue it. Don't wait for someone to tell you what to do (it may never happen). Instead, be curious, ask questions, and read everything you can. Although responsible for your training, your supervisor may not be prepared (or equipped) to help you every time you're ready to learn a new skill. A while ago, my administrative assistant decided she needed more challenging work and asked to prepare my next income tax return. Eager to be encouraging, I agreed to give her full rein over the project (especially since I had neither the expertise to train her nor a clue as to where to send her for instruction). Relying exclusively on tax software, as well as the IRS publications and web site, she took a stab and within weeks knocked out a near-seamless return. Not only did her efforts dramatically decrease my usual preparation fees, but she discovered ways to reduce my tax liability as well (my CPA's cursory review verified her accuracy). For her initiative, I gave her a well-deserved raise—one I won't *ever* let her forget!

Milk Your Journals for All They Are Worth

I know, I know—it's tough pouring through the stacks of magazines and newspapers that land on your desk. Yet trade publications are gold mines of action stimulators. Their purpose is to report what's new in an industry. Who's trying what? What's working and what isn't? You can't afford *not* to tap into this source.

Be Outspoken

Don't worry about appearing pushy or overzealous. Speak your mind with confidence. When you assertively communicate your ideas, the payoffs are often substantial. Simply assume others will respect your ideas, and you will immediately increase the chances of that being true. This doesn't mean you need to state your opinion on everything (we all know how off-putting *that* can be), but if you *do* have an insight and spot the opportunity, speak up. If you discover your observations were misguided, ask for clarification in order to learn from the experience. Generally speaking, however, always seek out ways to extend the authority and influence of your position. Consider your job description the general definition of your responsibility, not the boundary.

Study Someone Else's Job

Here's a superb way to demonstrate initiative: Make the time to learn a coworker's responsibilities, and your manager will see you in a league of your own (especially if you accomplish this on personal time). The added exposure will afford you insights into the workings of the company and may reveal other areas where decisive action can prove advantageous. How about becoming proficient at some aspect of your boss's job—and then offering to take it over? That kind of enterprising behavior is richly rewarded.

Don't Be Perfect

If you strive for perfection, congratulations; you're already miles ahead of your peers. If you expect to achieve it, however, you're on the wrong track entirely. There are two distinct approaches to excellence: *practical* perfectionism and *neurotic* perfectionism (can you guess which is preferable?). Neurotic perfectionists demand flawlessness, equating success with furthering the state of the art on every matter. This unrealistic, idealistic expectancy makes progress tortuously slow. (You may hear them say things like, "It's still not right—I'll have to come back and work on it more" or, "Keep at it—it's not quite there yet.") Finishing, of course, becomes virtually impossible given that it will *never* be perfect enough. As a consequence, the neurotic perfectionist's anxiety level is high and productivity is low. Without doubt, an unfinished masterpiece is worth much less than a perfectly adequate end product. Thus . . .

Be Practically Perfect

Practical perfectionism, by contrast, means committing to excellence, attending to detail, and adopting systematic, results-oriented work habits. It also means knowing when to say "enough." Fine-tuning a project the last 10 percent may require as much effort as the entire first 90 percent. Ask yourself if it's worth it—sometimes it is; sometimes it isn't. (An e-mail, for instance, is generally intended to communicate information, so a first draft usually suffices—just get your points down and send it off.) Therefore, when debating the benefits of producing higher quality in *any* endeavor, consider the time and energy required to achieve it. Look at it this way: Once you have completed one task, you've created the time and space in which to start another.

Don't Fixate on Breakthroughs

This trap can be just as debilitating as perfectionism. Don't sacrifice progress, however minor, waiting for the perfect result or situation. Avid initiators understand that a touchdown counts no matter how it is scored—both a yard-by-yard drive and one long-bomb pass will put six points on the scoreboard. Keep in mind that small strides are less risky, too, making it easier to gain support from others and redirect yourself should you veer off course.

Nudge or Tweak It

Those who take the lead seldom run a lap the same way twice. They know that some of the best proactive moves are minor, but new, improvements to old concerns. So think about the routine duties you perform, reports your write, and meetings you run. If you are like most people, you've stopped thinking critically about these activities—you're just on autopilot. Don't allow this to become a habit. Instead, make it a mission to do exactly the opposite—scrutinize everything you do. Determine how you could do it better or in less time, or even if you ought to be doing it at all (eliminating irrelevant work almost always yields a high dividend). Remember that empires have been built upon incremental improvements.

Cultivate Napoleonic Behavior

Once you have established yourself as a leader—and almost everyone is a leader in some arena—it's imperative you inspire others to make the first move. One method for accomplishing this is a military concept called "completed staff work," allegedly developed by Napoleon more than 200 years ago. When you worked under this famous French commander, you didn't approach him and say, "Sir, we have a problem. The supply lines are cut off. Ten thousand men are starving. What are we going to do?" Rather, you said, "Sir, we have a problem. The supply lines are cut off. Ten thousand men are starving. Here's what we can do. We can do A, we can do B, or we can do C. I recommend option B." In its simplest form, completed staff work means requiring that your subordinates communicate not only the problems, but also viable solutions as well as a clear recommendation. This approach is fundamental to your staff's assuming responsibility. Look at the advantages: First, it shifts the focus of those more interested in the dilemma than in the solution. Do you know people like that? They relish troubles and actually seem to delight in unnerving you with them. But if contributing workable resolutions is mandatory, people will dwell less on the obstacles at hand and more on overcoming them. Second, and as a consequence, completed staff work will yield more—and better—results. Let's face it: Because your team usually sits closer to the front lines, they will often see angles you don't. And, as a leader, you need as many options as possible.

Be Napoleonic Yourself

Completed staff work is also useful when you report to *your* boss. When you use this technique, one of two things will likely happen: (1) Your solution prevails and you earn a feather in your cap. Moreover, after consistently offering serviceable ideas, you might even say, "You know, boss, I've made the right call on this issue five out of the last six times. I feel I've got it down pat. Maybe I don't need to keep checking in with you." If he or she agrees, you may gain more autonomy and authority. Or (2) your proposal is off the mark, in which case you can learn from the experience: "Okay, boss, what did I miss? What do *you* know that I don't?" This situation just may prompt your manager to become a more impassioned and effective teacher.

Farm It Out

The individual who conceives a smart, serviceable idea is not always the ideal one to carry it through. When you lack the expertise—or brawn—to put your plan in motion, hire a professional. Or, if you simply have neither the time nor the financial means, delegate to the person within your realm (family member, friend, or coworker) who can best run with your concept. Either way, retain your control of the project while letting someone else (or a team) do the implementation. Initiating through others multiplies your productivity—and your results.

Job Share

Similarly, when you possess only a modicum of the essential skills and experience yet want to remain fully involved in the process, consider connecting with someone whose complementary talents can help you actualize your vision. Have you stalled on a particular component? Perhaps you need a partner. As the saying goes, "Two heads are better than one." (See Chapter 7 for more on why partnerships are powerful.)

Fail Proudly

Every new action carries a risk—some things *sound* great but don't work at all. Consequently, you'll be wrong a certain percentage of the time. But wrong isn't necessarily bad. In fact, you'll be in good company—superachievers generally have a long string of failures behind them. Learn to learn from your defeats. Consider this: If you are utterly in error, you get to experience the good fortune of colliding with information that will invariably set you back on track. And don't worry about your image. Look at the career statistics of professional baseball players. By and large, all-time home run leaders also sit atop the list of all-time strikeout leaders. But which stats do we remember?

Keep Your Passions Front and Center

In the absence of passion, starting *anything* becomes mostly hard work. We are motivated by what matters to us. In both life and career, identify those areas of inspiration—and steer relentlessly toward them. Soon you'll reach a place where ideation, execution, and results flow. In the final analysis, it is that innate illumination, not just exertion, that makes things happen.

Chapter FIVE

Dusting Off Your Dreams

Dream On

Dreams, as in aspirations, are considered by certain pragmatists to be frivolous indulgences . . . fantasies we shouldn't dwell on . . . the stuff of fairy tales and fiction . . . mere fluff. I'd argue that our dreams are the heavy metal of life. They represent the brass rings that give us reason to leap out of bed each morning. Our dreams mark our humanity by giving depth to our existence, and by adding dimension to what otherwise would be cardboard lives. Our dreams symbolize our blood and breath, infusing us with life and untold possibilities. Our dreams represent the gutsy, high-reaching personal ambitions that, in the end, separate lives worth living from lives simply having been lived.

Knowing your dream—and passionately pursuing it—will lead you directly toward your destiny.

Little Brother Jack the Jazz Pianist

In 1989, Michelle Pfeiffer was nominated for a Best Actress Oscar for her portrayal of Susie Diamond, the hooker turned torch singer, in the movie *The Fabulous Baker Boys*. The other two actors in the film are real-life brothers Beau and Jeff Bridges, playing Frank and Jack Baker, respectively.

In the story line, Jack and Frank are musicians in a two-grand-piano club act, playing mainly second-rate hotels and cocktail lounges. Earlier in their careers, their dual performance had been a crowd-pleasing novelty. But 15 years later, their show is getting stale and audiences are dwindling. In an attempt to revive their popularity, the less talented but more business-minded older brother, Frank, suggests adding a female vocalist. Jack reluctantly agrees.

During 37 pathetic but hilarious auditions, no singer emerges as suitable—until sexy Susie Diamond arrives late, and with an attitude. She pleads for one last tryout and then stuns the boys with her euphonic voice. Susie wins their favor and joins the pair.

Immediately, club patrons take notice of the new and expanded act featuring Diamond as the sultry chanteuse. Club owners clamor to rebook them, and the waning duo is suddenly resurrected into a thriving trio. As one might expect from this Hollywood story, a romance develops—and it's between Susie and Jack. That's when the act begins to fall apart.

All along, Jack, the truly gifted one, has been merely going through the motions at each performance, "hating every minute of it!" as he eventually screams to his big brother. Jack has become disgusted with himself for playing tired classics such as "Feelings" night after night. He longs to play more inspired jazz as a solo performer, but lacks the backbone to walk out on his brother and give up a steady paycheck. Frank, in turn, has a family to support, takes his responsibilities seriously, and wants to maintain the status quo.

Susie soon gets discovered and is lured away to sing more lucrative corporate jingles. The night before she plans to announce her departure from the threesome, she catches Jack playing his heart out in a neighborhood bar. The next evening, when in an after-show, back-alley exchange Susie tells him she's leaving, his apparent indifference causes her to lash out: "While Frank Baker was putting his kids to sleep last night, little brother Jack was out dusting off his dreams. . . . I was there . . . I saw it in your face. . . . I had you pegged as a loser the first time I saw you, but I was wrong. You're worse. You're a coward."

Susie Diamond, no longer "in the rough," does abandon the troika; Frank decides to teach piano lessons to neighborhood kids; and Jack accepts smaller gigs—"riding the keys" in a local club. The ending is bittersweet as Jack eventually reconciles with his older brother and then makes up with Susie.

When I first viewed this movie, I was struck by Pfeiffer's credible *My Fair Lady* transformation from call girl to diva, and by her insights into both Jack's character and his cowardice. In the end, she is the one who sways Jack to reach for his dream of playing *his* kind of music in *his* own way.

Each character had a dream—Susie to sing for a living, Frank to spend more time with his family, and Jack to play the music he loved. By the end of the film, all of their dreams were on the verge of being realized. In one way or another, they had all dusted off their dreams.

Throughout my life I've witnessed many people gather the courage to break free from their routines, rekindle their hopes and dreams, and then find a way to realize them. Here are some of their galvanizing stories.

David the Denver Firefighter

I hired David from a job ad we had posted in the student center of the local university. He was a freshman, just 17, and became my company's ninth and youngest employee. We needed someone to pack boxes, and he needed spending money. As the company grew and the years passed, he rose to become a front-line supervisor in our distribution center. He was sociable, extremely productive, and totally dependable. Although a bit self-effacing, David was liked and respected by all who knew him.

One day he came to me with a special request. Actually, it was more of a pronouncement. He informed me that even though he liked his job, his true calling was to be a firefighter, not a warehouse supervisor. David then divulged that he intended to test for one of the two openings in the Denver Fire Department. He also told me not to worry—there were more than 4,500 applicants for these two positions, so the odds of him landing one were remote. And even if he did get hired, he promised to continue working for us part-time. I was a little disappointed and a bit skeptical, but decided to support David in his quest, since he had given me six solid years and was instrumental in the building of our business.

A few of our senior managers even coached David on his interviewing skills, and we all gave him our moral support. We were full of encouragement as he prepared for the battery of tests he would face, but most of us doubted his chances of making the cut. He surprised us. Not only did he get the firefighter job, he kept his word and continued his employment with our company until the year I sold it. (Firefighters generally work two 24-hour shifts per week, so they have the time to hold second jobs.)

Sixteen years later, at 40, David has received three promotions, rising to the level of captain. He has fought countless fires and saved many lives, and he is a highly regarded member of the fire department. As of this writing, he heads a crew that is responsible for all structural, medical, and aircraft emergencies at Denver International Airport. Someday, he may have a shot at being the fire chief.

David is an example of someone who not only took advantage of his 20s, but stayed with a dream until he realized it. He could have remained in his comfortable job, earned decent money, and eventually made it to middle management. Instead, he refused to abandon his ambition—pursuing his fantasy job of becoming a firefighter and landing the brass ring. Although David made this vocational change fairly early in his career, he initially spent five years contemplating and preparing for it. He demonstrated a courageous spirit by striving for an occupation that was both dangerous and difficult to secure.

Bob the Transported Attorney

Bob was my company's primary attorney from 1982 until I hired in-house counsel in 1992. He won many cases on our behalf, kept us legally shipshape, and was central to the genesis of our company. Over time he built a prosperous practice in Denver specializing in intellectual property rights. Although we called him Big Bad Bob because of his tough legal tactics, he was, and is, an incredibly warmhearted and generous person (some might say, rare qualities in a lawyer!).

I've stayed in regular contact with Bob mainly via a book study group in which we've both been members for 15 years. In 2000, Bob dumbfounded our group by announcing he was closing his practice and relocating to upstate New York. For years he had been longing to move back to his hometown of Thousand Islands, near Syracuse. He missed the magnificent seasonal changes; he missed the water on the Saint Lawrence River; and he missed his old friends. Likewise, he wanted to work fewer hours so he could enjoy his life more. To make the move, he accepted a position in a smaller law firm in his hometown, took a sizable pay cut, and trimmed his standard of living. It was a bold step and, as he told me, "one that turned out better than I could have ever imagined."

Since returning to his geographic roots, Bob has

been promoted to managing partner of his new firm and has regained his earning power in short order. What appeared at first to require an enormous economic sacrifice has turned into a wise career move and a near-utopian lifestyle. In Bob's case, the dream wasn't about fame or fortune. It was about a return to a place he missed and a simpler way of life.

Attila the Enterprising Entrepreneur

Attila (yes, his real name is *Attila*) was a political refugee from Iran who came to America in 1984 at the age of 26 with no job, no green card, and $200 in his pocket. Without family or friends in Boulder and needing to support himself, he took a low-level job at a small data-entry business. After a few months' employment, he overheard his boss setting up a job interview for a programmer position in my company's information services department. He brazenly applied for the same position himself, landed it, and established himself as a programmer extraordinaire. Within two years, he rose to become the director of the entire division, eventually managing a staff of 30 with a $1.5 million annual budget—quite a Horatio Alger success story, though it doesn't end there.

Despite his complete devotion to our company, Attila told me that one day he wanted to start his own firm. I arrogantly thought to myself, "Yeah, so does everyone else," and dismissed his dream. On his own time, however, in the early 1990s, he created an intracompany e-mail program specific to our Wang operating system. He even convinced me that we should market it to other Wang-based companies. So we set up a corporation, Midnight Solutions, splitting ownership between Attila and my company. For a short while, Attila thought he might have an opportunity to disengage from our organization and run his own shop, assuming the e-mail program would be commercially successful. Unfortunately, though he had built a solid product, Wang was failing as a company and its user base—our target market—was rapidly moving to other platforms. Midnight Solutions ultimately went nowhere, leaving Attila a little discouraged, but still with a great job to which he continued giving his full attention and energy.

In December of 1994, knowing that I was in the process of selling my training firm, Attila moved on to another company, but it turned out to be only an interim job. He stayed there two years, and then decided to branch out as an independent computer programmer. He did well for himself. Even though he had doubled his income, he quickly tired of the long hours, the nonstop deadlines, the isolation of working by himself, and dealing with finicky clients. It was time to "scratch his itch" to start a real company with a real product (beyond the custom programs he wrote), real employees (besides himself), and real earnings (other than his hourly billings). He decided to launch RegOnline.

Here's the rest of the story about Attila's determination to set up his own business: Just before founding RegOnline, he was offered a lucrative post with Arthur

Andersen. At Attila's request, I analyzed the pros and cons of the job proposal, and concluded it was a terrific offer—one he should definitely accept. The position had an impressive title, a high salary, plenty of vacation time, and a generous bonus opportunity. But to Arthur Andersen's and my disbelief, he turned it down. Attila had such conviction that starting his own company was the way to go that he sacrificed a "sure thing" for a "maybe thing." (Considering the demise of Arthur Andersen after the Enron scandal and the eventual success of RegOnline, he clearly made the right call.)

Attila's initial claim to fame was the registration processing program he created for my former company. It was functional, durable, and user-friendly, handling over a million seminar enrollments annually. He capitalized on this experience a dozen years later by crafting an online registration system (hence the name *RegOnline*) that can be invisibly linked to other web sites. The first two years were slow going as he worked out the kinks, added features, and struggled to procure clients. Profits in his tiny start-up were nonexistent, yet he persisted, unwilling to forsake his vision. By the sixth year, revenues exceeded $2.5 million and RegOnline employed 18 people. The company had acquired hundreds of clients and was turning a handsome profit.

What I find so astonishing is that venture capitalists would not consider financing Attila's company at the outset because they viewed it as a boutique Internet business that would neither grow nor become significantly lucrative. How wrong they were. Now, four years following the high-tech crash of 2000, RegOnline is experiencing explosive growth, and is an established organization with impressive earnings. Way to go, Attila! Your dream is well under way.

Gordon the Aviation Mogul

Gordon owned the company from which I purchased all of my car phones from the mid-1980s to the late-1990s. His company, Calling All Cars (catchy, huh?), took advantage of the cellular boom. Initially, it sold and installed car-mounted phones exclusively. Later, Gordon added handheld phones and offered calling plans. He targeted high-profile executives and professional athletes to gain credibility and generate word-of-mouth referrals. That was his niche market. He sold phones and plans to the Denver Broncos, the Denver Nuggets, high-visibility entrepreneurs, and CEOs of major corporations. He would also befriend them, take them to lunch when delivering a new phone, and subtly pick their brains on general business matters. His networking ability was second to none.

Gordon rode the wireless wave until cell phones and calling plans verged on becoming a commodity, causing his profit margins to erode. In 1999, he knew his business needed a fundamental change. It turned out to be a wholesale change—from phones to planes. From the time he was a child, Gordon's burning passion had been airplanes—flying them, owning them, and talking about them. He just never believed he could make a living marketing them until he heeded his clients' counsel.

In listening to the wisdom of his business-savvy clients, one point he heard again and again was the importance of recognizing when it's time to sell a dying business and move on to something else. The most common regret his clientele shared was that they hadn't made bold moves earlier in their careers. So with these revelations in mind, he concluded it was time to segue from the cellular to the aviation business, where he finally envisioned a way to convert his lifelong fervor into a livelihood.

Within one year of polishing his aeronautical dream, Gordon had sold Calling All Cars, established Air Assets International, and was ardently selling and leasing aircraft. Today, he's no longer slugging it out in the cutthroat wireless industry. Instead, he's on a career path that complements his most beloved hobby—aviation!

Dawn the Artful Artist

For six years, I sat on the board of directors for Boulder's unconventional arts facility, the Dairy Center for the Arts. During my tenure, I became friendly with a number of accomplished artists, including a talented woman named Dawn. Along with her bohemian appearance (she epitomizes the "Boulder artist" look), she is intelligently opinionated and impressively outspoken about all things art-related. She also has the distinction of being a full-time working artist who supports herself solely from her craft. This wasn't always the case.

Dawn's educational background is in the arts—initially, dramatic theater. For most of her adult life, she has earned at least a portion of her income from her artwork. Being a full-time artist, though, was always just her dream. During the first 20 years of her career, she attempted (sometimes successfully, sometimes not) to fit her art into various businesses, including selling batik (a wax-resist dye process from Indonesia) shirts at craft fairs and marketing women's and children's hand-dyed socks to wholesalers. Dawn's intention at that time was to insert her artistic aptitude into a commercial business model versus simply selling her fine art. It was a hit-or-miss proposition with some notable achievements, such as a T-shirt in the collection of the Smithsonian Institution. Although all of her art-oriented businesses proved viable, none lasted more than a few years. Why? Because these endeavors took her away from the creative process she loved, making it difficult for her to put her heart and energy into them.

Not until the late 1990s did she give up her final day job and make the leap to supporting herself 100 percent from her artistic creations—predominantly paintings and murals. Prior to that, she held a variety of jobs: waiting tables, doing data entry, peddling outdoor electrical signs, and even selling recycling services. Although art was unquestionably her passion, being able to pay the bills determined where and how she spent the majority of her working hours.

Her epiphany came in 1998 when she posed a critical, life-changing question to herself: "From this point forth, am I going to live by fear or by faith?" That is, fear that she would not make it as a working artist, or faith that she could. Dawn chose faith. After years of hearing that being an artist was not a responsible career choice, and that it was simply too tough to make a living at it, she ultimately ignored these warnings and *just did it.* She stopped listening to struggling artists whine about how difficult it was; she refused to accept our culture's attitude that you had to be a modern-day Michelangelo to survive as a solo artist; and she quit doubting that she could do it. In the middle of her life, she dusted off her dream and made a total commitment to it.

Was this transition as simple for Dawn as I'm making it appear? Hardly. She told me it was like being a trapeze performer who had to let go of one set of rungs to be in position to grab another. It was all or nothing. She is now walking the road toward faith, and although certain fears still linger in her consciousness, she has reframed them. On one hand, she must continually push back on them, so they don't crush her confidence and immobilize her. As she told me, "Fear is the best excuse in the world to not pursue your dreams—most people use it quite effectively." On the other hand, she sees some of her fears as signals—signposts of new directions she must take to advance her artistry. For Dawn, whatever she fears most is what she must do next. And at this point in her career, there's no turning back.

Jana the Cutting Cowgirl

Jana, a neighbor and good friend, not only reached for and captured a dream in midlife, she first had to overcome an intense fear to achieve it.

As a child in Texas, Jana frequently attended the Houston Livestock Show and Rodeo with her family. Although she found the events wildly exciting and entertaining, she never wanted to go anywhere near the horses. Secretly, Jana was petrified they might attack her. While she had never had any traumatic experiences with these creatures, she was afraid they would eventually jump a fence and assault her. So, for decades, she kept her distance from farm animals, and kept her severe apprehension to herself.

At 44, Jana became determined to face her phobia, while simultaneously embracing her adoration of horses. Having shot rodeos (at a distance) for years as an amateur photographer, she wanted to overcome what she eventually determined was an irrational fear. She just didn't know how to go about it. Her brief encounter with an unsympathetic psychologist proved unhelpful. The therapist's reaction to her fright was, "What's your problem? Just get on a horse and ride it." For Jana, that "treatment" didn't exactly work.

Several years later she was introduced to Gary, a young horse trainer and bull rider, who she felt understood her fears. After all, she reasoned, who could relate better to her solicitudes than a cowboy who puts his life on the line every day in the corral? Finding his demeanor to be calm and controlled, Jana placed her full trust in him. With Gary as a coach, she finally overcame her trepidation and found herself in the saddle. She's been riding ever since.

If it ended there, this alone would be an uplifting story of triumph over terror. But it doesn't. Jana discovered she had such a deep passion for these animals that soon she was competing in national equestrian events. Her specialty now is *cutting,* a spectator sport that evolved from ranch-hand work. Cutting involves sorting cattle in open pastures, or separating them from the herd. Jana has a natural talent for this form of riding, and has been practicing and perfecting it for several years now. What she finds so fascinating about the discipline of cutting is, "the modulated movement between horse and rider—when it's working, it feels like perfection." To her credit, she placed first, second, and third in the first three events she entered. Not bad for a novice. Since then, she has won numerous ribbons and awards, competing with longtime riders, professionals, and serious amateurs, both male and female.

As to any lingering fears, she said, "I still have a few. I've had my feet stepped on, but nothing broken. I've also been kicked by cattle, but I'm still riding." One of her remaining *rational* concerns is roping. As she put it, "You can lose fingers. You're talking about 500 pounds of cattle going this way and 1,000 pounds of horse going that way. . . . It's not one of my favorite things to do." She's still doing it, though. Also, Jana gets a bit apprehensive when another rider's horse gets loose in the cutting pen, and she won't go into a stall unless she knows the animal—but those are fairly rational fears as well.

In addition to training and competing, Jana cares for her four Arabian horses—bathing, combing, brushing, and babying them regularly. She also mucks out the stalls and drives the trailer—talk about fully espousing one's passion. Hardly a horse-show prima donna, she converted a dread into a dream. Keep ridin', Jana.

Unfulfilled Aspirations?

Can you relate to any of these people? Do you see yourself trapped in an occupation or lifestyle that isn't what you want? Do you have ambitions that have been lying fallow for years—or decades? Do you ache to break out of a rut and do something more meaningful? A dream that gets you fired up about possibilities, quickens your pulse, and strikes a little fear in your gut is worth going after. Unfortunately, too many people never muster the mettle to pursue their lifelong yearnings (and some simply don't know how to go about it). Whether you have a sole aspiration or several, your life *can* change.

In the following two segments, I present specific advantages of reconnecting with your deep-seated longings and the methods for going after them with gusto.

The Delights of a Dream Come True

You Won't Be Marooned on "Someday Isle"

Someday I'll do this and someday I'll do that. Who hasn't had this thought from time to time? You're always meaning to get to that certain career goal, travel to an intriguing destination, or take up a new hobby. But somehow these things remain stuck in the back room of your mind and never become realities. Imagine an old book you find in your attic. It's so blanketed with dust that you can't even read the title. Then you wipe off the jacket and discover it's a valuable original edition, a classic that you've always wanted to read. This book in the attic represents one of your unrealized dreams. But first you must clean off the cover before you can appreciate its importance to you.

Feel Alive Again

Remember the song "What a Feeling" from the movie *Flashdance*? I concede this is corny, but who does not sense the exhilaration Jennifer Beals experiences at the film's end when she auditions to that rousing music and those impelling lyrics? When you're chasing a dream, the exultation that comes from knowing you may actually capture it is invigorating. You feel energized about what you and your life can become. Similarly, when you know where your real aspiration lies and you act on it with everything you've got, you gain a deep inner satisfaction that lasts day after day. Indeed, your dream is the expression of your individual pursuit of happiness.

Become a Muse

When you're on fire about something, your excitement is wildly contagious. To borrow a classic Iggy Pop song title, you demonstrate a "Lust for Life." You light up a room, you're cool to be around, and you inspire others to "go big."

Other Good Things Fall into Place

This particular reward falls into the category of *that's just the way the world works.* When you're following your heart by attempting to become what you were meant to be, momentum builds, and things usually start going your way. After taking the first step, the second step often follows naturally. That's what happened to David the firefighter. First, he took an initial written examination that was akin to a college SAT (math, vocabulary, comprehension, etc.) and easily passed it. Then he took the test for physical agility and passed it, as well, with high marks. After that, he aced the physical strength test, scored perfectly on the polygraph, and cinched the general physical. Finally, he had made it through the rigorous examination process and was on his way to actualizing what began as merely a pipe dream.

Less Anxiety and Depression

In a June 2002 cover story, *Time* magazine reported that 19 million people suffer from anxiety disorder, labeling it as the most common mental illness in the United States. Post-9/11, many say it's a near epidemic. And depression ranks right behind anxiety. It seems too many folks are either apathetically dragging themselves out of bed in the morning or are too afraid to crawl out from under the covers. How to lessen the stress and fear in your life? Dust off a dream and immerse yourself in it. By becoming engrossed in a virtuous obsession, you can get your mind off worldly as well as personal problems. Your consciousness converges on possibilities, not difficulties. With your mind engaged in a passionate pursuit, you'll have less inclination to fixate on niggling nuisances and trifling troubles over which you have no control.

It's One Way to Make Your Days Count

Following your dream is the quintessential way to make your days add up to a lifetime of bliss. Many of us, in fact, have more than one dream. However, when you clarify which dream is the most meaningful one to pursue and give it your attention and energy, you'll be living a life that matters.

Paths to Pursuing Your Passion

Pick One

It's hard to concentrate on more than one dream at a time, especially if they are "want it more than anything" undertakings. If you splinter yourself striving for multiple marks, you may achieve nothing more than spinning your wheels and becoming frustrated. So select one dream, laser-focus your talents and energy, and give it all you've got—just as David did when he coveted the firefighter's job.

Quit Talking about It and Start Doing It

What is standing in the way of your dream? I talked about writing this book for months before I wrote a word. It wasn't until I sat down at my computer one day and actually began drafting sentences that I made any progress. Sooner or later, you need to move beyond the chimera, address your procrastination, and begin the activity. It doesn't matter what your dream is. At some point the time for talk is long past, and the time for action is now. Dawn and Jana came to this crossroad, and just started doing it.

Schedule It

A goal without a deadline is nothing more than a castle in the air. And if it doesn't get on your planner, it probably won't ever get accomplished. Bob did this with his decision to relocate. When he finally put the move date on his calendar, he closed his practice and hired a moving company. At that point, there was no turning back. You can do the same. Maneuver your dream out of the abstract realm and into the concrete by setting a date.

Don't Feel It Has to Make You Rich

There are those who never go after a big dream because they believe it must make them wealthy. I don't agree. Happy and comfortable generally beats rich and miserable (or worse, unfulfilled). Moreover, when people relinquish the notion that pursuing their raison d'être should concomitantly make them a fortune, they often feel freer to actually take it on. When you do something mainly for the money, you are likely to be disappointed with the results. Conversely, when you go after things that are in alignment with your values and mission, you're more likely to become financially secure. It certainly happened this way for Bob, David, Attila, Gordon, and Dawn.

Know What You'll Sacrifice

Some dreams carry a hefty price tag. For Jack Baker, it was giving up his established act and steady paycheck; for Attila, it was a cushy job with Arthur Andersen; and for Bob, it was the prestige and earning power of a private law practice. In all cases these individuals put their aspirations ahead of their bank accounts. They went out on a limb and took the plunge, knowing they might be compromising their financial security. To them, the dream was worth the risks. At the same time . . .

Don't Bet It All

Your dream *could* turn out to be merely a rainbow *without* a pot of gold. Or worse, it could be ruinous. An associate of mine kept rolling over his investment in a burgeoning industry and amassed a personal net worth of $5 million. Instead of taking a portion of his earnings off the table, he gambled it all on one dream deal. Absolutely confident the transaction would yield a high return (as had all the previous ones), he poured his entire net worth—not to mention two years of his life—into the venture. This time, however, it didn't pan out: His new business failed immediately and he lost it all (as in *every last dime*). Eventually he had to sell his home, and his career floundered for years while he tried to reestablish credibility in his industry. Game over. Cash gone. Years wasted. Rather than risk this fate, you could . . .

Make a Low-Cost Probe

There *is* a way to court a dream before you commit all the way: Try it for a short period. Set a limit on how much time and/or money you'll invest, and hold steadfastly to that limit. You might discover that after a month or two you're not as enthused or optimistic about it as you were initially. That's perfectly okay. Low-cost probes allow you to explore attractive opportunities without overcommitting. Cut your losses and move on to the next item on your dream list. On the other hand . . .

Don't Bail Out Too Soon

If your dream doesn't materialize as quickly and smoothly as you had envisioned, don't hastily cast it aside. When you expect too much too soon, disillusionment can overwhelm you, leading to apathy, a surefire recipe for depression and dream abandonment. So set realistic goals, be passionate but patient, and hang in there. When Attila's new enterprise was slow going, he didn't ditch it and return to consulting. Instead, he improved the product, refined and expanded his company's marketing efforts, brought in a partner with complementary talents, and stayed the course. Now, less than a decade after launching his initially sluggish business, he is well on his way to becoming a self-made multimillionaire.

Revive One

Perhaps you already have a dream that simply needs dusting off. As the author, artist, inventor, educator (and my friend) Todd Siler wrote in his inspiring book, *Think Like a Genius* (Bantam, 1997), "Many people start off with passion but lose their way. It could be a passion for doing excellent work . . . for beauty . . . for adventure and travel. . . . One way to rekindle a passion is to rediscover the things that first sparked it. What was it that turned you on, that made you glow with excitement and constantly want to return? When you can answer that, you'll begin to uncover the mysterious disappearance of your passion." Likewise, with a dusty dream, we must re-create the environment that initially ignited our interest and enthusiasm. If we can discover what blew out the flame and then remove that impediment, we open up the possibility—and probability—that our dream can be fulfilled. Whatever the state of your dream—conceived but not yet acted upon, lying dormant, or abandoned—it is imperative to regain momentum and keep going.

Chapter SIX

Nourishing Your Mind

When It Came to Me

Brains count more today than ever. With the metamorphosis of our labor force from industrial workers to knowledge-based workers, this has become acutely apparent. Moreover, education is now the cornerstone of personal growth and earning potential.

This chapter is about lifelong learning—expanding your mind through ongoing intellectual stimulation. Its genesis was a guest appearance I made in 1988 on *Geraldo Live*—back when most daytime talk shows were not focused solely on deviants. Geraldo was showcasing entrepreneurs under age 30, and I, along with several other neophyte company founders, had the privilege of telling my story on national television.

Before the taping, I was in the makeup room when Geraldo stuck his head in the door and introduced himself. We chatted for a few minutes, and I deduced he was not the obnoxious investigative reporter he was purported to be, but, rather, quite an amiable guy. In spite of this, I still feared the notorious, in-your-face questions for which he was known.

Just before we took our seats on the set, Geraldo met briefly with us in the green room. We were all on edge, anxious that he might take shots at our youth and challenge what we could possibly know about entrepreneurship at such an early age. To our surprise, however, he said, "My opening question will be, 'To what do you attribute your success?' " He added, "And I do not—I repeat, do not—want you to answer 'Hard work.' If you do, every last viewer holding a remote will click to another channel. Nobody wants to hear that success is really just about hard work. Say anything else, but don't say 'Hard work.' " It was the first time a journalist had given me a question in advance and then told me how not to respond. All of the guests, including me, panicked because the answer we would have given was "Hard work." Our thoughts raced as we mentally scrambled to conjure up a more original reply.

In the few seconds I had before the cameras started rolling, I realized that my entrepreneurial accomplishment, up to that point, had as much to do with my continuing education beyond college as it did with hard work. I was an avid learner throughout my 20s, constantly seeking exposure to new concepts and ways of thinking. I was intent on expanding my knowledge base by soaking up as much information as possible. That keep-learning attitude not only helped me grow intellectually, but ultimately lent itself to my company's financial growth. Geraldo never asked me the dreaded question, yet having to contemplate it made me see that my unceasing thirst for knowledge had much to do with my professional achievements.

My career was spent mainly in the training field—it was my undisputed calling. Having been responsible for the continuing education of 10 million people over a 20-

year span, I feel particularly passionate about its value. Thus, I want to hard-sell you on the payoffs for being a lifelong learner. By the time you complete the next section, I'm hoping you'll be committed to making that pursuit a more integral part of your being. The chapter ends with specific ideas on how you can incorporate continuous learning into your daily life.

Carrots for Cultivating Your Curiosity

Gain Exposure to Knowledge

Specifically, gain exposure to the latest ideas, insights, research, and skills that are available. Let's take book publishing as an example. R.R. Bowker, the leading provider of bibliographic information in North America, estimated that more than 175,000 new titles and editions were released in 2003—a 17 percent increase over the previous year (and that's in the United States alone). Seems daunting, doesn't it? Still, when you compare this number to the current U.S. population of 295 million, it's equal to just one book written for every 1,685 minds. Now, doesn't it seem that out of 175,000 published volumes, at least one might contain something you need or want to know? Books are wellsprings of ideas that enrich you both personally and professionally. Reading them exposes you to humankind's greatest wisdom, allows you to tap into others' minds and experiences, and, most importantly, motivates you to take action and try new things. Authors are generally people who have something worthwhile to say based on their own discoveries, judgments, and acumen. And I'm not just referring to nonfiction writers. Often you can learn more by reading a work of fiction. If you've read Ayn Rand's book *The Fountainhead* (Bobbs-Merrill, 1943), you know what I'm talking about. I learned more about contemporary architecture, and the mind of a gifted architect, from devouring this brilliant novel than I ever have from *Architectural Digest* magazine. And consider the marvel of being able to read. According to Alvin Toffler in *Powershift* (Bantam, 1990), "Simply to read was a fantastic achievement in the ancient world. Saint Augustine, writing in the 5th century, refers to his mentor, Saint Ambrose, the bishop of Milan, who was so learned that he could actually read without moving his lips. For this astonishing feat he was regarded as the brainiest person in the world."

Attain a Competitive Advantage

The most profound comment I've heard about learning and competitiveness came from Ray Stata, the former chairman of Analog Devices, Inc. (ADI). He once said, "The rate at which individuals in organizations learn may become the only sustainable competitive advantage, especially in knowledge-intensive industries." In other words, no matter what your occupation, the only way to stay ahead is to always learn more and learn faster than your competitors. The rewards can be substantial because you can gain a significant upper hand simply by increasing the rate at which you're exposed to new ideas. What can you do to improve your job performance? What more can you learn about your company's product or service? How can you upgrade the technical skills required to do your job well? What industry-specific publications could you be reading regularly to remain current in your profession? And what rewards are you denying yourself by not augmenting your knowledge and abilities? The best way to give yourself a distinct edge is to become a continuous learner. A steady search for sagacity will set you apart if for no other reason than you'll likely know more than the next person. Nice guys sometimes finish last, but smart ones often finish first.

Enhance Your Power

You've probably heard the expression "Knowledge is power." Yes, it's as old as the hills, it's trite, and it's a cliché. But it also signifies two critical things—opportunity and leverage. Having a key piece of information even minutes before your rival can spell the difference between success and failure in today's marketplace. If you look through American history, many of our highly accomplished political leaders and renowned entrepreneurs were largely self-educated. Adams (both John and his son "Q"), Jefferson, Lincoln, Franklin, Edison, and Ford were all prolific learners.

Raise Your Income

The bottom line (with a double underscore) is that those who learn most are generally compensated best. In other words, the most prosperous people are often the most knowledgeable within their field. Typically, doctors, lawyers, and commission-based salespeople are the highest-paid professionals. Consider what they must accomplish academically to get where they are. In addition to completing an undergraduate degree, physicians survive four years in medical school, along with two grueling years as interns and two more as residents. Following college, attorneys expend three additional years in law school, pass the bar exam, and only then are offered the opportunity to start at the bottom and work their way up. There's a lot of mandatory learning in the process. Although sales professionals are not always required to attend or complete college, it is essential they know their products and services cold. Moreover, they must keep current with their clients' needs to better serve them. That discovery process takes considerable time and attention. And sales mega-earners understand that to be among the best in their field, and to stay on top of their game, they must habitually glean knowledge. So learn, grow, and earn.

Become Inspired

Learning is a tremendous motivational tool. I consider enlightenment to be the real energizer of life. Raising your consciousness, continually learning more, and becoming smarter are nourishment for the mind—the same as food and water are for the body. Learning keeps you enthusiastic. It keeps you charging toward your dreams and goals. Personally, I get exhilarated after gaining a new insight or mastering a new skill. Learning is also a catalyst for action. I am constitutionally incapable of not reacting to fresh information. I constantly want to plug it in, figure out how to relate it to my existing knowledge base, and apply it to my life and work. And I don't think I'm much different from you. In fact, I believe that's the way human beings naturally function, whether they know it or not.

Spark Your Creativity

Learning something new can often engender solutions to your current challenges. Years ago, I was stranded in an airport and used the time to catch up on some trade newsletters. One was on direct marketing—in particular, catalogs. At the time, my company's marketing team was trying to conceptualize new cover ideas for our upcoming catalog mailings. The newsletter I had just read was coincidentally all about brainstorming catalog covers. Lightbulbs began flashing, and I conceived 10 cover ideas in just minutes. However, since they were back-of-the-envelope inspirations, I returned to my office prepared for the marketing team to shoot down most of them. They did squelch a few but we tested the rest; all but one proved viable. The learning process can trigger your creative juices, lead you to new revelations, and multiply your ideation. In addition, it gets your mind going and gives you momentum.

Retain Knowledge

Continuous learning reminds us to use our accumulated knowledge. We should probably spend at least 10 percent of our overall education time unearthing what we once learned and have subsequently forgotten. I frequently read articles and books on the same topic because I'm concerned that over time I'll forget what I already know. Sometimes I simply need a refresher. Or maybe some esoteric detail wasn't relevant to me when I read it the first time, but now it is; and when it's presented in a different light or with a new twist, it hits home on the second read. Ergo, I'm constantly recycling the fundamental information I need to know. It's the old "use it or lose it" mentality. It's paramount to reexpose yourself to information you deem important to keep it actively retrievable in your mind. Otherwise, it could become refuse for your gray matter's circular file.

Be a Resource

My former business partner, Jeff, and I have always maintained a special relationship outside of our professional endeavors. He serves as my political adviser, and I serve as his investment adviser. Confession: I don't always take the time I could to fully understand what's happening in national politics and world news. Instead, whenever I'm curious about a political situation, I go to Jeff. In addition to having a degree in political science, he's a political maven—a vacuum who takes it all in. He can tell you virtually anything you want to know about any politician, who is in and who is out of power globally, and who is at war with whom. Being an aficionado, he's a gold mine of information. And when Jeff wants help analyzing his investments, he comes my way. Being informed can make you a valued resource to your circle of friends and associates.

Extend Your Lucidity

In a May 14, 2001, *Time* magazine cover story on Alzheimer's disease, it was reported that, "an active intellectual life . . . may actually protect you from the effects of the disease. . . . People with the most education were most independent and competent later in life. . . . Exercising what brain capacity you have offers some protection [against Alzheimer's]. . . . Stimulating the brain with continuous intellectual activity keeps neurons healthy and alive." How's that for scientific evidence that perpetual learning is at the root of a long, lucid life?

Be More Interesting

The final payoff of continuous education is quite simple—it can make you a more interesting person. Years ago I read a slim book, *The Debt and the Deficit,* by Robert

Heilbroner with Peter Bernstein (W.W. Norton, 1989). I concede the title doesn't sound gripping, and that's why I had postponed reading it for two years. Prior to then, I was "economically challenged," in that I could not distinguish a debt from a deficit. I was clueless. When I finished, though, I felt like I could hold my own with any economist (on that subject, at least). And for the next two weeks, I impressed all of my friends and associates with my understanding of the U.S. debt and deficit. Consider your perennial education to be an insurance policy against becoming a bore. You'll be more enlightened and conversant on the issues of the day. If nothing else, you will gain a deeper understanding of how the world works.

Actions for Achieving Mental Fitness

Make the Time

Yes, your work and family obligations may seem overwhelming, but it's necessary to look at learning as an essential part of your job and your life. It is not just something that is good in theory; these days, it's a requirement if you want to stay current with social issues and remain competitive in the business world. You can make time for what's important. Sometimes you may even need to force-feed yourself with small doses of learning, at least to get off the mark. To that end, I urge you to carve a chunk out of each day. In order to find the time, you may need to minimize telephone and television time, rise an hour earlier, or combine learning with other activities. Otherwise, it will likely linger as nothing more than a good intention.

Schedule It

Add learning appointments to your daily planner. Block out periods to read trade journals, watch a documentary, skim a book on a favorite subject, or attend a continuing education program. Take reading time, for example. The majority of people I talk with seem to find time for reading only in bed or on airplanes—those rare occasions when they are not being constantly interrupted by ringing telephones, e-mails, and questions. That's why it is important to allot time, calendar it, and then keep the appointment. In his book *Digerati: Encounters with the Cyber Elite* (HardWired, 1996), John Brockman wrote, "Bill Gates of Microsoft, the richest man in America, makes the time to learn. He has a ritual of taking a couple of weeks off every year to read and think." Despite the vast demands on his schedule, Gates finds time for study and contemplation.

Develop a "Quota" Consciousness

A learning quota will enable you to demonstrate and make tangible your commitment to learning. Keep in mind this must be a personal goal. It's not something you do just for your boss or peers. Perhaps I'm too fanatical about it, but at the beginning of every year I decide on the number of books, audio and video programs, films, magazines, classes, seminars, conferences, and self-study courses I want to experience over the next 12 months. Then I create lists of numbered blanks divided into two categories: personal and professional development. Next, I determine what, specifically, I want to learn (or re-learn), and how many resources I believe I can realistically digest. I spend the following year filling in the blanks and keeping myself on track to meet my goal. Although this exercise may seem excessive to some, it will definitely keep you in a self-education mode throughout the year.

Set Up a Learning Center

Designate an area in your home for learning. It can be a shared spot, though it is best if it's personal—just for you. It should be a place where, once you arrive, you can easily click into learning mode. There are several essential components. It has to be quiet—no distractions, no interruptions, and no concentration busters (e.g., a ringing phone). A low-traffic area, such as a spare bedroom, works best. It should become a special place—a retreat—that you associate strictly with reading and studying. Since the designated spot should be comfortable, I recommend installing a favorite chair, preferably one with low arms to accommodate your reading posture. An end table or nearby shelves are helpful for storing materials. Also, use nonglare lighting, as it's less damaging to your eyes. Your center needs to be a relaxing place without being so relaxing that you fall asleep.

Equip Your Center

Your learning devices should be there: a laptop (with an Internet connection); a television and VCR or DVD player; an audiotape or CD player; and a dictionary. A high-tech, electronic alternative to a conventional dictionary is the Franklin Language Master, which is a combined speaking dictionary, thesaurus, and grammar guide. This compact unit significantly expedites the process of looking up words. It's also wise to have a method of recording your observations and insights, which can be as simple as using a pen and paper or a laptop. Or, you could upgrade to a more sophisticated, portable dictation machine. The purpose is to record your reactions to what you're taking in. That's when the real learning occurs—when you pause, cogitate on what you've absorbed, and then document it. This process allows you to fix concepts in your mind. So, consider recording whatever you want to retain and share. Granted, if you don't already have these tools, acquiring them will require an outlay of cash. Nevertheless, the return on your investment will be colossal.

Stock Your Center

The final component of your learning center is a wide variety and generous supply of resource materials including any type of information you want to consume. The format options include books, periodicals, newsletters, tapes, DVDs, and CD-ROMs. Your library, bookstore, and the Internet are obvious sources. Load up!

Create Your Own Personalized Magazine

In the mid-1980s, I began subscribing to every general business magazine and industry trade journal available. At the time, however, our company was in a major growth phase, and I just couldn't find the time to get through them. After a while, I had collected so many back issues that I used one entire spare bedroom to stockpile them. I did keep them stacked by title and in chronological order, but I wasn't reading them. One day, an associate sent me a clipping from a magazine to which I already subscribed. The article was directly related to my industry and was actually several months old. At that point I thought, "This is ridiculous. I get that magazine, yet I had to rely on someone else to bring it to my attention. I've got to find some way to get through all these periodicals." The solution was simple enough. The day each publication arrived, I would scan the table of contents and then tear out the articles that were of greatest interest to me. I tossed the rest. On completion of my skimming sessions, I would have a slim folder of personally selected articles: no more stacks of journals that overwhelmed and intimidated me; no more flipping through useless ads; and no more time spent on interesting but irrelevant articles (at the expense of critical ones). It's an effective culling method I use to this day.

Share Your Magazine

There are two supplementary benefits to sharing your magazine. Once you've read the extracted articles, you can (1) route, fax, or mail them to someone else or (2) copy and distribute them to people in your organization. When it comes to assimilating and distributing large amounts of incoming published information, this approach can be a huge time-saver.

Read Reviews

I think this is one of the best-kept secrets for processing mass media. Whatever newspapers and periodicals you read, always check out the review section. By reading the reviews, you're always aware of the newest releases. Be it music, movies, theater, or books, you'll know what's up-and-coming. Publicists time their promotional announcements to hit prior to the publication date because they want reviews to appear before the title goes on sale. Reviews can give you the viewpoints of qualified critics who are paid to convey their honest impressions. And, in most cases, they're good at it. Critics make their living comparing a new work of art, literature, or the like to established quality standards. Often, the reviews are entertaining and humorous, and occasionally more so than the work itself. Roger Ebert attained his stature as a movie critic because audiences tend to agree with his viewpoint. Through trial and error, you can discern which critics reflect your tastes. Yet another reason for reading reviews is that you can decipher the major themes of a work in about three minutes, and, as such, you'll have a good idea whether pursuing it is a worthwhile use of your time. Finally, it's fun to compare your impressions to those of professional critics. You can even save the reviews for future reference.

Follow Columnists

Syndicated newspaper columnists can help you develop your own opinions about various issues by offering valuable tips, advice, and insights. Look for those who write in styles you enjoy and on topics that are relevant to both your career and your interests. And don't just read columnists who think as you do. Pick one or two who frequently express contrasting opinions so you can compare differing schools of thought. When there is a controversial point of debate buzzing around the media, I try to read the interpretations of several journalists. It usually helps me keep an open mind and form a gestalt opinion of what is really taking place.

Get Only News You Can Use

It's vital to stay current with major news events because knowing what's going on in the world can help you both personally and professionally. Be sure to filter in only what affects your life and interests you. You probably don't need to know about who got mugged or murdered last night, so avoid the violent stuff that will just depress you. Also, resist multiple sources. Unless it's a political, economic, or national security crisis, you probably don't need several versions of the same story. It's a waste of your time. Instead, go for consistency, convenience, and value. Consider relying on the Web exclusively. All national newspapers and broadcast networks maintain free web sites, some of which can be customized. You can also use their search functions or set e-mail alerts to obtain only the news you deem pertinent. (Check out NYTimes.com, USATODAY.com, washingtonpost.com, WSJ.com, ABCNEWS.com, CBS NEWS.com, CNN.com, FOXNews.com, MSNBC.com, and PBS.org.) Don't spend too much time on this activity—15 to 30 minutes spread throughout the day will give you the headlines, and a little more.

Be an Auditory Learner

If you're already an audiotape or CD fan, I'm probably preaching to the choir. Audio programs are an efficacious way to put mental downtime to work. You can listen to instructional programs while you're doing other things like cooking, cleaning, exercising (at home or at your health club), and commuting. One of the best times to listen to audios is in the morning when you are grooming and getting dressed. Nearly all best-sellers are now released in cassette and CD formats, and many can be downloaded to an MP3 player. Most programs are available abridged, enabling you to glean just the highlights—a real time-saver.

Listen Smartly

As a seasoned audio learner, I offer you these four tips that I have found quite useful:

1. Strategically place your listening devices. Put a unit in your kitchen, one in your learning center, and another wherever you spend large blocks of time. A Walkman-type player is also a good option, especially if you're a runner or take long walks.
2. Periodically stop the program, and then take a minute to think about how you can apply the best ideas and make them work for you.
3. Eject bad tapes. My rule of thumb is if I'm not hooked within the first 10 minutes, out comes the tape or CD, and it's on to the next program.
4. Experience it twice. Relisten to a program for a second (or third) time until you squeeze out every last valuable idea.

Learn While You Drive

Create your own "university on wheels." For many people, this is the best way to build learning time into their day. If the commute to your workplace exceeds 10 minutes each way, it makes sense. But what if you prefer listening to music or talk radio in the car? Compromise. Save the talk or the tunes for the drive home after work, when it's time to unwind and relax. But on the way to work, listen to personal development tapes or CDs. It's a smart way to get yourself mentally ready for the day ahead. And taking a book on tape with you on a long road trip can be a revelatory experience. Time flies, and you'll be amazed at the enjoyment tapes can bring to the two-lane blacktop.

Revisit the Classroom

Attending seminars and workshops is a tried-and-true forum for continuing education. They offer you practical, up-to-the-minute information in a face-to-face environment. Moreover, these programs afford you an opportunity to ask an expert about issues meaningful to you, while teaching you skills and techniques for enhancing your life. Participating in training sessions is actually about working on yourself. In these settings, you transcend your normal state of mind and enter an idea arena where creative solutions to old problems can emerge. That's the real value of classroom learning.

Enroll in Something

A night class at your local college, a one-day computer course, a workshop on interpersonal communication skills, a weekend retreat on meditation, or a speaking appearance by a renowned author at your favorite bookstore—from time to time, commit to attending an educational event where you stand a chance of learning something insightful and useful.

Exercise for Your Mind

The best way I've found to read daily and stick with an exercise program is to do them both at once on a stationary bike. Every morning, my first activity involves spending 40 minutes reading and riding. My current bike of choice is a Recumbent Lifecycle, which is a comfortable alternative to upright pedaling—it's also ideal for reading while you pedal. I use a sheet-music stand to balance my reading material. To be honest, I'm not much of an exercise nut. In fact, I generally dread exercising because I'm not too crazy about the "no pain, no gain" trade-off. But I love to read. What motivates me to exercise at 6:45 each morning is not the alleged benefits of being in good physical condition. They are merely a by-product. Rather, the real incentive is to discover what happens in the next chapter of my current book selection! (I read only books on the bike—no magazines or newspapers—preferring to use my morning exercise time to whittle down my ever-growing stack of unread tomes.) I've stayed with this routine religiously for the past five years and have averaged 40 books a year—all read on my trusty and utilitarian Lifecycle. If you enjoy multitasking, this regimen is an efficient way to simultaneously exercise your mind and body. (You can also take in self-development programs while on the bike via audiobooks or training videos, but my clear preference is reading.) As former two-term governor of Colorado Richard Lamm once said, "Everyone has an hour in his or her day to exercise." Why not combine it with an hour of learning to maximize the time investment?

Start (or Join) a Book Club

Since 1991 I've been an active member of a reading group that has grown from six to ten members. Every other month, we meet for dinner and discuss a nonfiction book one of us has chosen (we take turns selecting books and hosting the meetings). In general, we choose titles that are tangentially related to the subject of leadership, falling within the categories of biographies, history, political memoirs, and personal development. A week prior to each meeting, the host e-mails our group a handful of questions to contemplate, which subsequently serve as discussion starters. Following a relaxing dinner in a private room at a local restaurant, we critique the designated selection, debate the questions posed, and then give personal updates. Not only do we share our take-away impressions of the author's message, but we also share a camaraderie that is now well into its second decade (I count my book-club mates among my closest friends). I credit my commitment to this group with forcing me to delve into challenging volumes I might not have otherwise, such as William Manchester's *The Last Lion* (Little, Brown, 1983–1988); Neil Baldwin's *Edison: Inventing the Century* (Hyperion, 1995); Nelson Mandela's *Long Walk to Freedom* (Little, Brown, 1994); and Richard Reeves' *President Kennedy* (Simon & Schuster, 1993). Deliberating on books of this caliber has proven an enormous educational and growth experience, broadening my worldview by listening to others' perspectives. If you don't already participate in such a group, I urge you to seek one you can join—or form your own. You'll find the intellectual stimulation and concomitant friendships invaluable.

Relate and Apply

The ancient Greek playwright Sophocles (496–406 B.C.) once said, "Alas, how terrible is wisdom when it brings no profit to the man who is wise." In other words, it's really a waste when you can't use what you know. This recalls the more contemporary saying that I refer to in the preface, "It's not what you know, but what you do with what you know, that counts." Don't settle for pedantic knowledge only; in the end, it's action that counts most. So always try to relate and apply the things you learn by considering how you can use them to improve your life.

Write like Willard

One of my all-time favorite seminar stories brings the previous point to life. I'm borrowing this account from Mike Vance, who once held the title Dean of Disneyland University, and who now speaks internationally on the topic of creative thinking. Once he was giving a lecture and J. Willard Marriott, the founder of the Marriott Corporation, was sitting in the front row. Throughout Vance's presentation, Marriott (who at the time was in his 90s) was taking copious notes—with both hands. As this was somewhat peculiar and distracting, Vance paused in midsentence and said, "Excuse me, sir, what are you doing?" Marriott finished what he was writing, put down his pens, and tilted his head upward. He then responded slowly, "With my right hand I'm writing down what you're saying; with my left hand I'm writing down what I'm going to do about it." Pretty profound, isn't it? I'm not ambidextrous, so I can't employ this eccentric note-taking technique. Instead, I try to jot down just what I might do with whatever information is being presented. Unless you can write with both hands, I suggest you consider doing the same.

Try Them All

Experiment with each of these techniques until some become habitual. Doing so will put you in a permanent state of learning just like a professional athlete who is always in training—in season and off. Whether you're a scientist, a construction worker, or a homemaker—if you want to become better at your craft, make continuous learning a way of life. After all, it's ultimately up to you to take responsibility for your education. To that end, transform yourself into the most informed person you can be and commit to reaching a new level of everyday erudition, starting today.

Chapter SEVEN

Rising above the Mean

Why We Need to Stand Out

Please be clear: This chapter is not about our need to be the absolute best, or even to be in the top 20 percent. Rather, it is about our self-requirement to be on the right-hand side of the bell curve; not settling for average or for doing the minimum just to get by. It's about our innate longing to stand apart, to jut above the masses, and to be noticed.

Ernest Becker, the late cultural anthropologist, psychologist, and sociologist, posthumously won the 1974 Pulitzer Prize in the nonfiction category for his book *The Denial of Death* (Free Press, 1973). In his magnum opus, Becker describes a paradox that explains man's basic yearning to simultaneously "fit in" and "stand out."* The following excerpts, which I have quoted liberally, elucidate his cogent theory:

> *[This] paradox takes the form of two motives or urges that seem to be part of creature consciousness and that point in two opposite directions. On one hand the creature*

---

*For you trivia buffs, *The Denial of Death* was the book Alvie (Woody Allen) purchased for Annie (Diane Keaton) in the 1976 Academy Award–winning film *Annie Hall.*

[man] is impelled by a powerful desire to identify with the cosmic process, to merge himself with the rest of nature. On the other hand he wants to be unique, to stand out as something different and apart.

In describing man's eagerness to fit in, Becker writes:

The first motive—to merge and lose oneself in something larger—comes from man's horror of isolation, of being thrust back upon his own feeble energies alone; he feels tremblingly small and impotent in the face of transcendent nature. If he gives in to his natural feeling of cosmic dependence, the desire to be part of something bigger, it puts him at peace and at oneness, gives him a sense of self-expansion in a larger beyond, and so heightens his being, giving him truly a feeling of transcendent value. . . . The person reaches out naturally for a self beyond his own self in order to know who he is at all, in order to feel that he belongs in the universe.

In recounting man's need to stand out, Becker continues:

[Man] can expand his self-feeling by . . . the other ontological [relating to being] motive Eros [the god of love], the urge for more life, for exciting experience, for the development of the self-powers, for developing the uniqueness of the individual creature, the impulsion to stick out

> *of nature and shine. Life is, after all, a challenge to the creature, a fascinating opportunity to expand. Psychologically it is the urge for individuation; how do I realize my distinctive gifts, make my own contribution to the world through my own self-expansion?*

He summarizes this concept of contradiction:

> *Man thus has the absolute tension of the dualism. Individuation means the human creature has to oppose itself to the rest of nature [stick out]. It creates precisely the isolation that one can't stand—and yet needs in order to develop distinctively. It creates the difference that becomes such a burden; it accents the smallness of oneself and the sticking-outness at the same time.*

Since my first exposure to Becker's brilliant, although illogical, contention 20 years ago, I have witnessed its truth in every aspect of human endeavor, from familial to recreational to professional pursuits. Some obvious examples: We want to be the favorite child, but also be considered an equal sibling. We long to be the most popular kid in school, yet at the same time we yearn to be just one of the gang. We itch to be the revered boss and still be welcome at any table in the employee lunchroom. We fantasize about being a world-renowned rock star, though we insist on preserving our privacy as an inconspicuous member of the community. In essence, we seem to crave both extremes.

Even Max Agrees with Becker

From infancy on, we are influenced by parents and authority figures to "be our best." Consider the title song from the popular Disney flick, *The Goofy Movie,* which embraces Becker's "fit in/stand out" thesis. In an effort to win the respect of his classmates—and the attention of his favorite girl—Goofy's son, Max, performs a lip-synched rendition of the song "Stand Out." To his jam-packed high school auditorium, he dances and sings:

Some people settle for the typical thing,
Livin' all their lives waitin' in the wings.
It ain't a question of "if," just a matter of time,
Before I move to the front of the line.

And once you're watchin' ev'ry move that I make
Ya gotta believe that I got what it takes. . . .

To stand out above the crowd,
Even if I gotta shout out loud.
'Til mine is the only face you see,
Gonna stand out 'til you notice me.

With this mind-set—and a little help from Dad—Max eventually wins the respect of his schoolmates and gets the girl. All because he makes the decision to rise above the rest.

While I'm obviously borrowing from Becker's concept of "absolute tension" (once again, concurrently melding in and sticking out), from here on the discussion focuses mainly on the "stand out" aspect. First, I present two illustrations of its potential impact; then, I offer my thoughts on the prizes and proven practices for moving beyond mediocrity.

The Recompense for Raising Your Average

Here's one of my favorite examples of doing better than average, with its concomitant rewards. Although it's a baseball analogy, it's easy to follow and the math is simple.

A batting average equals the number of hits divided by at-bats. The typical number of official at-bats for a starting player in a major league season is about 500. To have a batting average of .250, a player will need 125 hits for those 500 at-bats (125/500 = .250). A solid .250 hitter in the majors would probably play 5 to 10 seasons and make $1 million per year—with a good agent. Before the player reaches his 10th season, however, he'll likely be replaced in the lineup by an up-and-coming rookie, demoted to the minor leagues, or released (i.e., cut from the team). And five years later, few will remember what teams he played for—or that he even played pro ball.

If this player can raise his lifetime batting average to .300, his story will be much different. He'll probably make several million dollars per year (possibly tens of millions), start in the all-star game season after season, and regularly see his name in the sports-page headlines.

Five years after retiring (and he'll be the one to decide when it's time to call it quits), most certainly he will not be forgotten. Rather, he'll be elected to the Baseball Hall of Fame in his first year of eligibility.

Do you know the difference between hitting .250 and .300? It's only 25 hits per season—just one extra hit per 20 at-bats. It doesn't seem like that much, does it? It isn't (only 20 percent more hits), but the rewards and fame are often 1,000 percent greater. When all is said and done, to be paid and recognized at a significantly higher level, a professional baseball player does not need to double or triple (bad pun, sorry . . .) his efforts and results. Instead, he just has to try a little harder and hit a little better.

The same is true for you. Raising your average can give you that extra edge toward becoming a .300 hitter in your life's work. And if you achieve it, the compensation and éclat will follow.

Fore! Kane Is Coming Your Way

He hails from Down Under, but someday I suspect he'll be known the world over. His name is Kane Webber, and he's an archetypical example of how actually hitting *below* average can catapult you out of obscurity and give you a shot at glory.

Kane was the number-one-ranked member of his collegiate golf team and named an All-American. Now, as a recent college graduate, he is vying for a spot on the

Professional Golfers' Association (PGA) tour. Although he considers his chances only about 60 to 70 percent, I'm confident he'll make the cut. Here's why.

From an early age, Kane's love for golf and strong will to succeed have dominated his life, earning him many titles and accolades. And his self-discipline is remarkable. Throughout his high school days, he practiced seven days a week, rising early each morning to hit balls for an hour before classes began, a training routine he continued into college. Every day, he worked on his swing, emphasizing the weaker part of his game (putting), while keeping the strongest part (mid-irons) sharp. "I still spend a disproportionate amount of practice time on the shots I need to improve—that's my focus," Kane explained. He has positioned himself to rise above other golf-pro wannabes by understanding the critical importance of developing every aspect of his sport.

I asked Kane how much of his ability is innate, and how much comes from practicing and playing daily. He told me that without the latter he would probably have an 8 to 10 handicap (most recreational golfers would kill for that). With the time and effort he has invested in refining his technique, however, he now maintains a "scratch" (or zero) handicap—well above mediocre.

Another attribute that sets Kane apart is his ability to purge distracting thoughts from his mind and stay focused. That sounds like a common trait of all fierce competitors, right? Perhaps, but he takes it a giant step further. Case in point: The day after his father's funeral, he honored his dad's wishes and kept his commitment to play in a local tournament. Despite his intense sorrow, he managed to keep his attention on the contest and stunned the field by shooting a 59 (12 under par), including a hole in one. Do you know anyone who can conjure such astounding concentration in the midst of grief? I don't.

Given that 72 is par for most golf courses, I queried Kane on how he views his various scores above and below that mark. He thought for a moment, and then responded in his strong Aussie accent, "If I shoot above par, I know I could have done better, and I'm usually disappointed. If I shoot 70 to 72, I rate it a good day. Any score that begins with a 5 or 6 gives me a fantastic feeling." Kane is acutely aware of how superior—and inferior—play affects him. Moreover, he understands what he must do to stay ahead of the field and realize his dream of becoming an elite PGA contender.

In the summer of 2002, Kane won his first major tournament, the State Stroke Play, which is considered one of the most prestigious amateur titles. But he didn't start out with a blistering round. Hardly. On the first hole, he scored a disastrous quadruple bogey (4 over par). Unfazed, he realized he still had 71 holes left to play and vowed to "win back those extra strokes." And he did, finishing one stroke ahead of the runner-up. Skill and self-assurance were his allies in victory.

Kane told me that the key to his future success is "pushing his mind" (i.e., gaining the confidence) to believe that he can make any shot at any time. As he put it, "It's like sinking a three-foot putt on the last hole. . . . I've done it a thousand times before, and I know I can do it again." He already has that degree of certitude with much of his game and is determined to develop it with the remainder. No doubt he can—and will.

And, in your own way, so can you. I will now share my thoughts on the considerable rewards of going above and beyond as well as the best practices for distinguishing yourself by excelling.

Perks of Transcending the Ordinary

Fame

Granted, notoriety may not be important to everyone, yet it sure is nice to be spotlighted as someone who is a standard deviation (or more) above the norm. When you stand out above the crowd, generally you are recognized. You may not receive a million-dollar salary and be featured on the cover of *People* magazine, but you may well earn a promotion, a raise, a bonus, or accolades in your company and/or association newsletter. It's a question of degree, but ascending above the masses will certainly get someone's attention.

Fortune

When you're a notch above in any endeavor, the financial compensation is not always commensurate with the degree of improvement above the median. Just like the earlier .300-hitter baseball analogy, the rewards can be pleasantly disproportionate with results. "A little better" often (though, I concede, not always) translates into a whole lot more monetary gain. Our society puts an immense premium on above-average performance, making it advantageous, to put it mildly, to strive for excellence.

Pride

We gain justifiable self-respect for both our efforts and our accomplishments. I consider self-regard to be the ultimate motivator—we naturally want to feel good about ourselves. When we know we've given our best and outperformed the average expectation, our self-esteem and self-worth are heightened. I believe this to be a universal truth of human nature, and the most compelling argument for being all we can be. Ah, the self-satisfaction of a job well done.

Admiration

As a corollary to pride, transcending a so-so level of performance is a surefire way to get people to treat you deferentially. We revere those who make a name by rising above the multitudes. If you want to be lionized (or just acknowledged), do better than average—in your job, in a volunteer capacity, in athletic competition, or as a parent.

Emulation

When we raise our quality and quantity standards, others pay attention and try to match our higher contribution. And in doing so, we positively influence and inspire our children, our peer groups, and our community. So, set an exemplary example.

Linkage

Moving beyond mediocrity connects to the other topics in this book—harvesting your bonus decade, making your days count, overcoming procrastination, taking initiative, dusting off your dreams, nourishing your mind, and dealing with your disappointments. If you are consistently exceeding medial performance, you'll have an easier time implementing all the other life-enhancing precepts.

Modes for Moving beyond Mediocrity

Do One Thing and Do It Well

Avoid splintering your ambitions and you'll avoid diluting your achievements. Ben (not his real name) is a paradigm of how fractured aspirations can lead to mediocre attainments. Ben is an individual-sports enthusiast, and every year he switches to a different one. When I first met him, he was into bicycling, then windsurfing, and now, of all things, juggling! Just when Ben starts to get good at one sport, he gets bored, quits, and takes up another. I've always believed he would feel more gratification by sticking with one athletic endeavor until he mastered it. You probably know friends and colleagues who change careers every couple of years. They seem to be constantly starting over, barely achieving a modicum of expertise in any one field. For whatever reason, they grow bored, get discouraged, become critical of management, or feel unchallenged, causing them to walk away prematurely. The next occupation, they always say, is the one they'll stick with. Seldom does it happen that way. The lesson: Find where your true talents and opportunities lie, and then *stay in that space* (at least until you "get good").

Have a One-Track Mind

When asked how he had accomplished so much throughout his life, Winston Churchill responded, "Because I think about only one thing at a time." Don't clutter your mind. Stick with your current objective until you achieve it, and then move on to the next one. By taking a linear approach, you'll go further, faster.

Get It Down, Then Get It Right

Just get started and worry about fine-tuning later. My first boss, Rick, said this to me repeatedly. Whenever I started an assignment and he sensed I was procrastinating, unsure how to begin, or making the project a bigger deal than it really was (thus letting it overwhelm me), he would tell me to forget about getting it right. Instead, he would encourage me to "just knock out a first draft." After I had moved off dead center and finished the initial go-around, Rick would then urge me to keep reworking it until I was satisfied with the end-product. The notion of ignoring perfection at the outset and striving for it at the end was a revelation. But now it makes total sense to me. Think about your memorable accomplishments. I bet the really stellar ones were the result of continual rethinking and refining until you got them just right. And even then you probably came up with another tweak to improve upon it. Whether it's an A+ term paper you wrote back in school, an insightful analysis that impressed your manager, or a new system that saved your company time and money, it likely wasn't achieved on your first try.

Practice Pragmatic Perfectionism

Don't be an obsessive perfectionist to the point of never finishing. Do, however, acknowledge that those who accomplish superior feats tend to conduct themselves more like perfectionists than settlers for "good enough." The personal luxuries our economy has to offer—an intelligently designed home; a sleek, head-turning sports car; a cup of Starbucks coffee; a pair of comfortable 501 jeans; or a piece of Godiva chocolate—were all the brainchildren of pragmatic perfectionists: people who did not achieve perfection, but came close (all right, maybe the Godiva folks got it perfect!). Keep your perspective and be a perfectionist within the realm of practicality.

Demand Self-Discipline

Ask yourself: Where do I have it? Where do I lack it? And how can I train myself to have more? Without willpower, it's hard to break away from the pack. As the song goes, "What the world needs now is love, sweet love. It's the only thing that there's just too little of." The same could be said about self-discipline. So if your self-control wanes, have a heart-to-heart with yourself. Sometimes that's all it takes to get back on track.

Advertise Your Ambitions

Post your list of goals in a prominent place, keeping them front and center. This can be awkward since your aspirations are often personal and private. Yet by displaying them where you will encounter them regularly, you'll be reminded of what you're going after. Share your intentions with the expectation that, once you announce your plan, you had better do it. Consider this technique self-imposed peer pressure. As Erma Bombeck once wrote, "It takes a lot of courage to show your dreams to someone else."

Develop Your "OP"

OP stands for "own program" and involves doing what you know you must to extract your personal best when it counts. It also requires understanding how you attain peak performance, such as advanced training regimens, mental-preparation exercises, and performance-day rituals. This is how alpine downhill racer AJ Kitt prepared for World Cup competitions (you'll read more on AJ in the next chapter). Spend time contemplating and recording what, exactly, you are doing when you find yourself delivering your best.

Become a World Authority

I can't recall where I saw this statistic, but it was an eye-opener: If you read five books on any one subject, you can consider yourself a global expert of sorts based on everyone else's relative knowledge. Five books is all it takes, so pick a subject and start reading carefully.

Study the Masters

Whatever your interest (e.g., career, hobby, sport, etc.), identify the high achievers in your league. Put them under your microscope and study their every move. Emulating a top dog is a wonderful way to leapfrog over the competition.

Experience It Twice

As a society we are preoccupied with the latest and greatest. Whether it's software, CDs, books, movies, or fashions—you name it—we are overly eager to check out the newest stuff. When you take the time to reexperience a quality work, however, you often gain more from the second exposure than from the first. For instance, every year or two I watch my all-time favorite movie, *East of Eden* (which launched James Dean's short, but brilliant, acting career). Why? Because I find it enormously entertaining, and I always unearth previously overlooked symbolism. Each viewing leads to a deeper understanding of the plot and characters, which, in turn, brings more enjoyment. The same can be said of great works of art, literature, and even financial reports. If you want an edge, take a second, closer look at whatever you want to grasp more fully.

Learn to Burn

Be able to concentrate at will. By pinpointing your energies like a magnifying glass on a dry leaf, you achieve your deepest level of intensity and impact. Some term this skill the ability to "flow," while others call it being able to "laser-focus." I call it "learning to burn," and it's all about your mind, body, and soul converging on a specific objective. It may require a special location, a quiet (or white noise) environment, a certain time of day, or meditating before you can mentally get there. If you know the hows, whens, and wheres of your concentration prerequisites, you can usually tune into "crank mode" when you must.

Partner Up

The complementary skills of two people working in sync can often produce "more and better" than you could on your own. Would the Beatles have achieved living-legend status without the songwriting partnership of John Lennon and Paul McCartney? Did Art Garfunkel do much after Paul Simon went solo? And how big would the Ben & Jerry's brand be without both Ben's *and* Jerry's involvement? I never could have built CareerTrack without the considerable contributions of my partner, Jeff. If you're having difficulty making a mark, consider taking on a partner with complementary talents.

Find the Extra Hour

The extra hour is there. You just have to ferret it out. You may have to rise earlier or use your lunch break for something besides eating, but you can find 60 minutes to spare. Another hour each day equates to 365 hours, or more than two weeks, of extra productivity per year. The individuals who march ahead of the crowd understand the difference this can make. When you're tempted to waste time oversleeping, watching the "idiot box," or doing a frivolous activity, consider allocating that time to a more worthwhile endeavor—even if it's just solitude.

Stay Healthy

It's up to you to determine the foods you eat, how much (or whether) you exercise, the amount of sleep you get, and what substances you abuse. For me, sugar is the vice of choice. I don't care a whit about alcohol, tobacco, salt, caffeine, or nonprescription drugs. But take away my sugar supply and I'm not a happy fellow. I know it causes cavities, diminishes my energy, and keeps my waist two inches larger than I'd prefer, but I love the stuff and would rather moderate than eradicate it altogether. You know your own indulgences, dependencies, and bad habits. The question is, can you eliminate or limit them?

If you want to be "better than the average bear," living healthier is a great place to start.

Know What You'll Sacrifice

What is it worth to be a cut above? What price are you willing to pay? It could be working long hours, traveling constantly, enduring physical pain, forgoing a more lucrative career in another profession, having no spouse and/or family, missing your kids' activities, or putting up with more stress and enjoying less relaxation. Get clear on the costs of being super at something. Then decide if it's worth it. If it is, pony up. If it isn't, don't forfeit your desire to excel—just lower the bar a bit.

Chapter EIGHT

Dealing with Disappointment

The Price of Expectations

Poet and essayist Alexander Pope (1688–1744) sardonically noted, "Blessed is the man who expects nothing, for he shall never be disappointed." Ah, if we could only live that way. In reality, though, we all have expectations, hopes, and dreams. Consequently, we all experience disappointments. They come in many forms—from minor to major, from temporary to long-term—and affect everyone, regardless of age, wealth, or social status. Yet, whatever their nature, setbacks can be overcome, or at least resolved, without completely immobilizing us. The following true stories illustrate the ways in which four individuals coped with their disappointments.

The Alpine Jet Blown Off Course

AJ Kitt is one of America's all-time great downhill racers, being the first male U.S. alpine skier to have competed in four consecutive Winter Olympic Games. He was on the cover of *Sports Illustrated* and featured in *Men's Journal*, starred in two Warren Miller films, and was the main character in *Right on the Edge of Crazy*, acclaimed as the best book ever written about ski racing. When AJ declined to reveal what the initials AJ stood for, a sports journalist nicknamed him "Alpine Jet" for his turbocharged downhill speed. In his skiing career, which started at the age of two, AJ faced significant challenges, victories, disappointments, and rebounds. This story is about the adversities he faced, how he managed, and what he learned.

His parents, peers, and coaches knew AJ had a something-special ability when no instructor at his local ski resort could beat him in a top-to-bottom, all-out challenge. And that was in 1981, when he was only 13. After attending two of the premier ski academies during his high school years, AJ made the U.S. Ski Team at age 18. From there, success came fast and furious, with top-10 finishes becoming expected. In December of 1991, AJ won the season-opening race on the famed Val d'Isère course in France and graced the top of the winners' podium. It was America's first World Cup victory since 1984. By the end of the 1991–1992 season, at the pinnacle of his career, AJ was ranked third in the world.

In December of 1992, AJ again scored the best time in the Val d'Isère World Cup, only to have the race stopped due to a sudden snowstorm. Even though the top-seeded racers had already run the course and placed behind him, there was an unwritten rule regarding the number of starting skiers needed for an official event and, in this case, that number was insufficient. Politics got in the way, and AJ was denied the coveted first-place Crystal Trophy. He did receive the prize money, though, which tells you something about how "canceled" the race really was. As much as AJ was upset about the outcome, he accepted that these things happen. He shrugged it off and bounced back a week later with a third-place finish in the Val Gardena World Cup in Italy.

In March of 1993, AJ won the Aspen World Cup. Or so he thought. Despite warm, sunny weather (too warm, in fact), the results were nullified due to a dangerous rut that had developed near the bottom of the course. Instead of repairing the defect and allowing the competition to continue (which is the standard operating procedure), Federation of International Skiing (FIS) politics prevailed, and the contest was called off even though the required number of skiers had already left the starting gate. AJ was denied the victory and the accompanying World Cup ranking points. As consolation, however, he did receive the $30,000 purse. Despite this, AJ was more than disappointed this time; he was outraged. Two days prior to the race, he had pointed out that the placement of an extra gate would cause this rut and suggested its removal. He was told by the senior official (who did not welcome racers' input) to mind his own business or risk disqualification. Ironically, even though he had predicted the course defect that developed, AJ's invalidated first-place finish and the corresponding points forfeiture in actuality made him the most penalized competitor. Worst of all, the unawarded points cost AJ a second-in-the-world ranking that season, which negatively impacted his overall standing and results for the next several years. To put it mildly, the outcome wasn't fair, and he felt let down. And, pardon the pun, things went downhill from there. Unfortunate circumstances and a series of injuries became all too common for AJ.

In March of 1995, despite a blizzard-like snowstorm on race day, AJ again clocked the best time in the Aspen World Cup. Unfortunately, the 31st skier crashed, suffering a compound fracture. At that point, the course was deemed unsafe, and the race was halted. According to new FIS rules, however, because more than one-third of the field had started, the results were official—that is, until the French and Canadian teams lodged a protest a week later. (The top French racer would have lost his number-one world ranking due to his slow performance, and the Canadians wanted to rerun the race for their younger, back-of-the-pack skiers who hadn't been allowed to participate.) Once more, AJ received the prize money and, this time, the trophy as well, but no points. The third time was anything but the charm as he came to the realization that life isn't fair, and people don't always play by the rules. Things were never quite the same for AJ after that annulled victory.

In December of the same year, AJ had a violent accident on a training run and blew out his left knee. It was his first serious injury. Although thwarted for the remainder of that season, he vowed to come back. He did, but not to his prior world-class form. As he told me, "It was like having a head-on car collision resulting in a serious injury. From then on, you realize how dangerous driving can really be—you drive a little slower, you don't run yellow lights, and you're more careful behind the wheel." The same is true with downhill racing. Though he skied smarter after the accident, he wasn't as fast as he had been. The memory of the smashup, combined with his no-longer-perfect knee, kept AJ from skiing optimally—that is, "right on the edge of crazy."

In 1998, AJ skied in his fourth and final Olympics at the Nagano Winter Games in Japan. In the prerace training runs, he'd skied fast, finishing in the top three on consecutive days. On race day, which had been postponed a week due to snowstorms, his time was even better. After the first few gates, he was in the lead. At the sixth gate, however, he did what one-third of the field had done—he skied too fast and missed it. Unbeknownst to AJ, the officials had moved the sixth gate up-mountain to decelerate the skiers and make the course safer. The only problem: No one had informed the racers or their coaches. Because inclement weather had threatened to cancel the race altogether, there was no time to alert everyone and repeat the inspection process as FIS regulations normally dictated. As one Olympic official later confessed in private, "We just wanted to get the race in." Although he skied at breakneck speed, AJ, along with many of the other top seeds, "DQ'd" (was disqualified). I was there. I saw it—another heart-wrenching letdown for the Alpine Jet.

After retiring in 1998, AJ turned pro and was teamed with 1994 Olympic downhill gold medalist Tommy Moe to represent the United States in the Ford Downhill Series. In a training run before the season's first race, AJ caught an edge and wiped out, fracturing his right wrist in three places. While he did manage to return for the final race, he forfeited considerable publicity and prize money by missing most of the season. Bad luck and foiled aspirations continued to haunt him.

What kept AJ from giving up after these repeated setbacks? "First and foremost, I still had the desire to win. I'd been at the top of the sport before, and I wanted to get there again. It wasn't the money or the awards, but the chance to be the best in the world that kept me coming back. Second, I didn't know how to quit. I wasn't raised to be a quitter. It was my constitution to keep trying."

How did he handle the anger and despair caused by these disappointments? "It was tough. I won't tell you I wasn't discouraged and down at times. After my first World Cup victory was denied, I considered it insignificant in the big picture of my career. I was still confident and determined. After my second and third triumphs were invalidated, I started to wonder if this sport was what I thought it was. I had always assumed that if I gave my best and placed first legitimately, I would be recognized and rewarded. But I discovered that there's more to winning than meets the eye—like money, drugs, and politics. I learned that all I could control is how hard I trained, what I put into my body, the technical soundness of my equipment, and how fast I skied. If I went all out and won, great; if not, I'd dust the snow off my butt and take another run."

Blaine's Heartbreak

Blaine knew something had gone awry, but he never expected Leah to call off the impending marriage *and* the relationship. It didn't happen overnight. As he put it, "The distance growing between us was gradual. And a tension had been developing for months—I could feel it coming to a head."

She broke it off the day before moving back to Southern California, where she had grown up, where he had lived after college, where they had met, and where they had intended to marry and settle down. Blaine had planned to join her once he had tied up loose ends and lined up a new job. He thought they could work it out, reasoning, "I knew we'd become a little distant, and things weren't like they used to be. Maybe we just needed some time apart to mend our differences." Instead, she'd told him she wanted a clean break. The full force of their severed romance hit him immediately.

Then he went numb.

Blaine shut down and isolated himself. After all, "It was too awkward and uncomfortable to talk about, and the people willing to listen probably wouldn't have understood, anyway. The hardest part was having no one to talk to." For several weeks, he spiraled down into a dark space, feeling very alone and stuck in the pain.

At best, his outlook appeared bleak. Having already been married and divorced once, Blaine had been both skeptical of—and grateful for—a second chance at a committed relationship, a loving marriage, and a close-knit family. It had always been his consummate dream. But Leah's surprise split confirmed his skepticism, dashing his hopes and leaving him distraught and disillusioned. Now, his dream seemed unrealistic, unattainable, and just not meant to be. In Blaine's words, "Once I emerged from the fog of the shock, I took stock of my life. I needed to heal, but it was much easier said than done." He decided to proceed with his own migration to California and put what energy he could muster into planning the move. He also contemplated what to do with the rest of his life. Having given up his job and most of his possessions, Blaine realized he had a clean slate for starting over. In an effort to pull himself out of his doldrums, he recommitted to his life goals and relocated.

A month after getting settled, Blaine called Leah to reconnect and see if there was any hope of reconciliation. Anything but, he learned. Adding insult to injury, she told Blaine over the phone that she would never have feelings for him again. He was left crushed and angry. Crushed for an obvious reason (little chance of getting her back) and angry because he realized that perhaps she had never loved him (and that he had wasted his time on the relationship). How could they have been so close and then suddenly "over with"? Soon after that "Dear John" phone call, though, Blaine actually started feeling better. He was no longer down on life in general—just upset with her. As he recalled, "It was easier when I was mad than when I was depressed to acknowledge that it was probably over."

In actuality, Blaine never fully recovered. He had accepted that they were no longer a couple, though he hadn't given up hope that someday they might get back together. "I wasn't holding a candle, but I wasn't ready to move on, either. . . . I never completely let go." His biggest concern, however, was that he'd never get another chance at the happiness he sought.

Not all love stories have happy endings; this one did. Four months later, Leah called Blaine out of the blue and asked him to go surfing. He was confused by her invitation and still felt angry, but accepted out of curiosity (and maybe some lingering wish that absence had made her heart grow fonder). The day went awkwardly, and when he asked to see her again, she declined. Blaine assumed Leah was afraid of leading him on when he didn't hear from her soon after. A month later, though, Leah called and asked him out on an official date. This tryst led to the rekindling of their passion and, ultimately, their reuniting.

Sensing Leah was as lost and confused as he had been, Blaine sent her *The Alchemist* by Paul Coelho (Harper San Francisco, 1995), a book about "the transforming power of listening to our hearts." It had helped him deal with their breakup, and it obviously impacted her as well, because six months later, Leah asked Blaine to marry *her*. He said yes, and within a year they exchanged vows.

Although Leah's initial withdrawal had proven a wrenching rejection, Blaine had grieved his loss and shifted his focus to other parts of his life. He reclaimed his goals, put his career back on track, and made a fresh start. Had he forever wallowed in anguish, Leah may not have returned to him. I guess the old saying rings true: "That which you give up, you gain." Or expressed another way, surrendering your attachment to a certain outcome may actually allow it to happen.

MS for Life

In his junior year of college, my fraternity brother and roommate, Skip, was diagnosed with multiple sclerosis (MS). To say the least, he was devastated by the news. At the time, Skip was just 20. He was athletic (especially adept at skiing and golfing); handsome (he dated the prettiest girls); smart (he studied less than I, but had higher grades); and fun loving (a party was always more amusing when he was there). The world was in his palm—until the MS was detected.

Skip's initial reaction to the diagnosis was, "Guys like me don't get MS. I have no time for it—there are too many things I want to accomplish with my life. I won't let it hold me back." He vowed not to let it affect his daily activities or control him in any way. Headstrong and filled with youthful exuberance, he believed he could conquer the disease. When I asked him what he meant by "conquer," he shot back, "Not end up in a wheel chair, bedridden, or visibly disabled." Even though he clearly understood what MS could do to his body, like Superman, he appeared invincible.

Despite Skip's Christopher Reeve-like optimism, the MS soon took the upper hand. Skip's athletic skills deteriorated, and he went from having a six handicap to being nothing more than a "hack golfer," as he put it. No longer having the strength or balance to negotiate the slopes, he eventually gave up skiing altogether. Also, he started experiencing weakness in his limbs, as well as chronic fatigue. With the loss of energy and decline in his health, he realized not only that the MS was real, but that his body was succumbing to it. (Multiple sclerosis erodes the human body much like kryptonite debilitates Superman's strength.)

Still, Skip put on a game face each day and willed himself to carry on. When people asked how he was feeling, he would often silently equivocate and then exclaim, "Tremendous!" Even though he felt terrible, he believed that if he replied enthusiastically, he should act that way, which often resulted in his *truly* feeling better. This "fake it till you make it" coping method helped him get through the initial fatigue and despondency.

After living with MS for a few years, Skip moved to Hawaii. Having finally acknowledged that he had a debilitating disease, he wanted to live independently, fearing that someday his girlfriend and parents might not be around to care for him. Moreover, he needed time away to figure out how to salvage his MS-affected life. In Hawaii, he accomplished both ends. He embraced a holistic health program—changed his diet, exercised regularly, and adopted other health-enhancing practices. Most importantly, he learned to accept and deal with his situation.

Two years later, Skip returned to his hometown. Despite his healthier lifestyle, his physical capabilities had slipped noticeably. His limp and inability to walk extended distances made it apparent to family and friends that the disease was having an adverse impact. As he told me, "The most challenging facet of MS, initially, was seeing others view me differently, even though I was still the same person albeit in a slightly less functional body. That was—and still is—a tough one." He sometimes feels as if others see him as a malady rather than as a whole person. Since Skip lives his illness every minute, he appreciates it when people ignore his occasional symptoms. He reflected further, "MS has changed my life so dramatically because it's changed my perception of who I thought I was. Yes, I was dejected at first, but early on I learned the cliché, 'time waits for no one,' and I realized it wouldn't wait for me. I had to buck up and move on. Heck, you'd do the same." Perhaps, but I'm not so confident I could muster Skip's courage and perseverance.

With the acceptance of his fate and his resolve to live a normal life, Skip married and had a son, became president of a prominent local bank, and is still the life-loving guy I knew him to be years ago. Twenty-five years later, he has started skiing again and returned to the golf links in spite of his ongoing MS challenges. He decided that participating in sports, even at a reduced level of agility and intensity, beats surrendering to his condition. He has found a new form of joy in simply taking part versus having to be among the best. His return to athletics was also prompted by his desire to model determination to his boy.

When asked what he has learned from living more than half of his life with multiple sclerosis, he thought for a moment and responded, "No matter what setback life deals you, continue to *try, try, try*." His words reminded me of Winston Churchill's famous nine-word speech, "Never give up, never give up, never give up!" You didn't, Skip.

No Appointment . . . Big Disappointment

A respected attorney for two decades and a trial court judge for five years, David was considered in a poll by his peers to be the most qualified nominee for an opening judgeship on the state supreme court. However, when the governor appointed another candidate, David was distressed, but not surprised. Strong lobby influences combined with an affirmative-action mandate had prevailed. Nonetheless, the governor urged David to reapply for the next vacancy, emphasizing how important it was to both the state and to him personally. With positive expectations, David did just that.

Would the governor pass him over *again*? Surely not. The first time David had been nominated as a trial judge, he had been ranked as the most qualified. Nevertheless, the same governor chose another nominee. Embarrassed, the governor admitted to David that, politically, his hands had been tied. Still believing in David's superb credentials, he encouraged him to reapply for the next vacancy. Within two years he had attained the trial judge appointment.

With high hopes for changing the judicial system to make it more accessible, expedient, and fair, David accepted a second nomination to the supreme court. Judges and lawyers statewide again rated him the most capable candidate, and governmental insiders and bar leaders assured him he had a lock on the state's highest appointment. At long last, this would be his time.

Evidently not.

The governor had written each nominee and specifically forbade stumping for the position. David steadfastly followed that directive, but a less competent nominee launched an unprecedented, covert campaign. And it worked—despite violating the no-politicking edict, his opponent walked away with the highly coveted judicial appointment. Once again, politics had prevailed over fairness.

David wasn't merely disheartened—he was devastated. He had played by the rules. Yet a process held up to the public as merit selection had been corrupted, subverted, and converted into the "same old politics." He resolved never again to apply for the supreme court. A full year after his unforeseen rebuff, he confided, "This has been a year of recovery . . . of trying to overcome a deep and tenacious depression . . . of appreciating the severity of the impact all this has had on the rest of my life." He went on, "Nothing cuts to my core like unfairness . . . and it hasn't helped that rationality and merit have been my keys for creating a sense of control in a world that feels constantly out of control."

Eventually, David gained some relief. Upon reflection, he realized that he had been afforded important life lessons. He had been given a rare glimpse into the inside workings of politics, and without compromising his own principles. Yet he learned so much more on a deeper level. He noted, "As President Carter simply, but profoundly, stated, 'Life is unfair.' Similarly, Buddha recognized, 'Life is suffering.' It is how we respond to the suffering that matters. And that response must come from growth within. At least I emerged from the black hole with my sense of self and my values intact."

David also took time to evaluate his future. He thought about what the mythologist Joseph Campbell once said: "Follow your bliss." David realized how much he had enjoyed his work in mediation before he had sat on the bench. Although he was anxious about the risks involved, he decided to leave the court and reinvent himself. Today, he is a successful, independent, professional mediator and arbitrator. "I'm back to my real passion—helping people solve their legal problems *before* the court system has squeezed them dry—financially and emotionally." No, he's not on the supreme court, but the monetary and psychological rewards of following his passion far surpass what David had envisioned possible. He now wryly quotes a song by the Rolling Stones: "You can't always get what you want, but if you try sometimes, you just might find you get what you need."

Just as David finally came to terms with circumstances outside his control, so must we all. And as the good judge's wife sagely pointed out, "Good guys *can* finish first. You just have to redefine winning." In the following two sections I present meaningful advantages of learning to cope with disappointment and clear routes to initiating a comeback.

The Dividends of Dealing with Downers

Coping Capability

To the extent you are actively willing to address your setbacks, you'll be more psychologically armed to handle reversals of fortune, lapses in judgment, other people's mistakes, unpredictability, chaos, and turmoil. This way, the next time you're dealt a bad card, you'll have a better sense of how to play it.

Experience, Judgment, and Wisdom

It's an ancient, but classic axiom: "Bad judgment leads to experience; experience leads to good judgment; good judgment leads to wisdom." Disappointment isn't always rooted in your bad judgment, but generally *someone's* clouded thinking is responsible. When you make a poor decision that causes you distress and regret, don't miss the accompanying lesson to be learned. Setbacks can breed sapience.

Revelations

Big disappointments often lead to big revelations. For example, let's say you are passed over for a significant promotion you both expect and believe you deserve. If given a legitimate reason—one you understand and agree with—you can examine your role in what became the decision. With that insight, you can clarify what you must do, moving forward, to further your career. Then it's possible to come back from the comedown. An epiphany is frequently found in unexpected, inauspicious circumstances.

Revived Momentum

When you confront a discouraging situation, you can be freed from the coinciding, immobilizing thoughts that surround it. And if you come to terms with the unfortunate (and, hopefully, temporary) turnabout, you may experience rejuvenation and renewed determination. An associate of mine put his business on hold for several years while he worked his way up the leadership hierarchy of a prestigious international business organization. He hoped eventually to be named president, but, instead, ended up the number-two pick in his final year of eligibility. Although he was crestfallen over having given so much of himself only to end up "second to one," he did not regret the effort. Rather, he accepted the outcome and rechanneled his time, energy, and enthusiasm back into his own business. Sales increased by 50 percent within a year. He used the second-place finish as an impetus to revive his company, putting it solidly back on a growth track.

Demonstrated Mettle

Leaders routinely discover ways around roadblocks. It's how they earn respect and attract followers. When you can consistently move past the awful stuff that gets randomly thrown in your path, you are seen as a person who can overcome obstacles, a seasoned pilot who can fly passengers out of the storm and to safety. When life dashes your plans, try to see it as an opportunity to show resilience and garner respect.

The Silver Lining

Is there any inherent good in what's making you miserable? That's a serious question. Somewhere in the terribleness of your ill-fated predicament, can you identify something that just might work out better than anticipated? The promise of that possibility can ease your despair. Force yourself to find the hope that lies at the bottom of Pandora's box—it's there.

Mental Buoyancy

Face a letdown squarely, and you'll be less inclined to sink into an abyss of despair and inertia. If you ignore it or allow it to fester and consume you, however, your élan vital will stagnate, or worse, deteriorate, leaving deep scars that may never heal. Conversely, if you address setbacks head-on, you can retain clarity for assessing your go-forward options. By utilizing the suggestions in the next section, you can spring back from the downers in life, and stay mentally afloat.

The Routes to Rebounding

Give It Time

Your flight was canceled an hour after the scheduled departure, the airline lost your luggage, you left your wallet somewhere in the terminal, and your car was towed from the airport parking structure. It's now a month later—do you still care? Time helps abate most upsetting situations. The mental devastation of a titanic disappointment also diminishes with time, but requires patience. Even Judge David acknowledged, "A recovery process that should have taken months actually took me years." Eventually, though, he did gain perspective, which helped to reduce the harsh impact of the governor's decision.

Dial Your "911 Buddy"

Call a close friend to talk out what's troubling you, and to elicit empathy or sympathy. To the extent you tap your support network, you'll ease the dejection that often accompanies sunken hopes and unmet expectations. Case in point: At a festive social gathering, a close friend, Steve, pulled me aside and asked for 15 minutes to vent. Just prior to the occasion, he had attended a court hearing where the judge (not David!) had made an ill-advised ruling, and *not* in his favor. Steve was distraught and needed someone to just listen while he recounted the judge's uninformed decision. Steve was something to see. He mocked the judge, replayed the "he said, she said" attorney exchanges, and got himself all worked up over his displeasure with the outcome. Steve was really getting into dramatizing the event. Even though I couldn't make his troubles disappear, I could see that he felt better after having let loose his anger and frustration. If nothing else, it was cathartic.

Sulk, and Then Get Over It

We certainly need to grieve our disappointments, but at some point enough is enough. It's not always easy to put on a happy face immediately after a defeat, yet we can't saddle ourselves with crushed feelings forever. We must give ourselves time to wallow in a negative space, knowing that eventually we will have to snap back, or at least move on. Blaine certainly hung *his* head for a while until he realized he had to go forward with his life, regardless of whether it included Leah.

Quit Asking "Why?" and Find the Answer

A relative's mother dwells on the "whys" surrounding each adversity she experiences. "Why did this happen to *me*?" and "Why is this happening *now*?" are her two favorite "poor me" mantras. These self-pitying questions don't help her situation, nor does adopting a victim mind-set. Instead, she needs to find ways to recognize what she *can* control and what she *can't.* Meanwhile, it would help her to recite the "Serenity Prayer" (which is really a plea) that is popular in Eastern philosophy and widely quoted in 12-step programs: "Grant me the serenity to accept the things I cannot change, the courage to change the things I can, and the wisdom to know the difference." Amen.

Analyze It

A good dose of introspection can teach you volumes about how you may have participated in an unforeseen setback. The next time bad stuff hits you from out of nowhere, get to the heart of it. Try to be as inquisitive and objective as you are dispirited. Ask yourself not *why,* but *how,* as in "How did this happen?" AJ routinely did this after every missed gate resulting in disqualification, every crash that caused him injury, and each annulled victory that cost him ranking points. It helped him to understand what role he played, if any, in his own misfortunes.

Dig Deep

Archaeologists excavate the earth to learn about past civilizations. The farther down they dig, the more they discover how humans and animals once lived. Those who delve deeper generally learn the most. Remember this analogy whenever you're attempting to understand your response to disappointing news. Probe into the depths of your psyche to see what's going on in there and why you react the way you do. Do you blame others? Lash out at loved ones? Self-medicate with alcohol, drugs, or food? Isolate yourself? Your reaction to disheartening events will certainly influence how you handle them. Take a good, honest look at yourself. If your reactive behaviors are extreme, consider seeking professional help to learn healthier ways to deal with future disappointments.

Journal Your Feelings

Writing can help you understand and let go of disenchantment. After the sale of my company, I left on good terms with all but one senior executive. Although she and I had worked in simpatico for years, we clashed regularly in the weeks leading up to the closing. Because we never had an opportunity to reconcile our differences, I wrote her a long letter to explain (and apologize for) my behavior—and to convey my frustration with hers. For legal and confidentiality reasons, my attorney wouldn't permit me to mail the letter. Just drafting it, though, aided me in getting beyond my distress over our strained relationship. Trust me, ranting on paper is quite efficacious.

Face the Facts

Is an impediment you recently suffered a sign to be honest about certain aspects of your life? Are you living in denial over a relationship that isn't working, a job that isn't right for you, or a negative circumstance that keeps repeating itself? What's the disappointment telling you? Are you trying too hard or not hard enough? Are you doing too little or too much? Are your expectations too high or not high enough? Come clean on these questions, and the answers will reveal truths that will help you grow.

Act "As If"

Sometimes you have to feign normalcy to expedite your recovery from a blow. If you act as if the status quo is restored or as if the lingering mishap has subsided, healing and higher spirits will come about. Skip effectively used this method to lift himself out of the initial melancholy following his diagnosis. When he felt poorly, he behaved as though he was well, and frequently he *did* feel better. So take a lesson from Skip—avoid moping and act as if things are better (or at least getting better).

Step Backward, Then Forward

When your letdown results from a missed opportunity or failed objective, use the ill fortune to reenergize yourself and try again. Don't see it as a reason to capitulate; rather, reframe it as the one step backward you must often take before you can take the next two forward. If nothing else, bounce back for your team, work group, or family because they count on your resiliency. AJ Kitt was considered the unofficial leader and captain of the U.S. Ski Team in part because of the mature manner in which he handled his bad luck.

Focus Forward

As Judge David expounded, "It's not always possible to resolve our disappointments. We must recognize that some wounds heal and disappear, while some leave pain and scars." Indeed, sometimes our defeats hurt us so deeply that they cause permanent damage. Yet we *can* decide to move ahead despite the ache. It's not about forgetting; it's more a matter of shifting our focus forward. Ultimately, we control how much or how little our setbacks imprint our future. David was devastated by his second failed attempt for a seat on the supreme court and still has painful memories. Nonetheless, he eventually chose to look ahead to other possibilities and now, in a new way, is assisting others through the legal labyrinth called our justice system.

Dwell on All That's Good

When things go awry and you become unhinged, force yourself to think about the other 95 percent of your life that's perfectly fine. Take an inventory of what's still working, how satisfied you feel in other areas, and all the things for which you can be grateful. That will help you isolate the negativity and put it in perspective. It may sound Pollyanna-ish, but it's a good habit to develop. And remember this: Most disappointments are temporary takedowns, not cataclysmic disasters.

Afterword

Evergreen Wisdom

Encapsulated here is the essence of my thoughts on how to move forward in your life—purposefully, constructively, and enthusiastically.

- *Harvest the Bonus Decade*—No matter your age, exploit that "extra 10."
- *Make Your Days Count*—Remember, you have a finite number, so add meaning to each one.
- *Triumph over Procrastination*—Get off the dime and get to it.
- *Make Things Happen*—Take charge, set the pace, and pioneer progress.
- *Dust Off Your Dreams*—Drive your destiny by renewing aspirations.

- *Nourish Your Mind*—Make continuous learning the cornerstone of personal and professional growth.
- *Rise above the Mean*—Move beyond mediocrity and stand apart.
- *Deal with Disappointment*—Rebound from setbacks and move on.

Drawing from experiences (my own and others') spanning more than four decades, I chose these topics for their enduring nature. They were relevant 20 years ago, and they'll be just as pertinent 20 years hence. As you progress through life's various stages, look to *Make Your Move*'s ageless advice as an ongoing source of guidance and inspiration.

Did You Mine *Make Your Move* for All It's Worth?

Contemplate what you've read. Which passages resonate with you? What meaningful take-aways come to mind? Which recommendations made you think, "I should do that"? Have you noted them? If not, flip through the pages, scanning headings for the precepts that stir you to take action. Better yet, put a check mark next to each one you'd like to integrate into your daily life. Then, as a visual reference, make a list to keep them ever present, thereby increasing the likelihood of their actually being implemented.

Once More, with Feeling (and a Marker)

Are there sections or specific suggestions you promised yourself you would revisit? As I advocated in Chapter 5, experience it twice. If you're not ready now to turn back to page 1, consider rereading *Make Your Move* in six months for reinforcement. And if you didn't on the first go-through, underline or highlight what's meaningful and jot down your observations in the margins. Dig deeper the second time around, extracting every last idea that will propel you toward positive change.

Pass It On

Is there counsel within you'd like to share? That's my hope. I wrote *Make Your Move* to disseminate my thoughts on achieving a fuller life, and I'm eager to accomplish that end. One way to assimilate a specific recommendation is to talk about it—with family, friends, and colleagues. In sharing an idea, you crystallize it in your mind while elevating your commitment to incorporating it. So don't hesitate to pass along anything you believe will benefit others as well.

Most Importantly, Get Unstuck

It happens to all of us. We hit lulls and grow complacent, or worse, we reel from setbacks and find ourselves completely off track. But, in truth, identifying a new direction is never more paramount than when we're feeling most unfocused and adrift. As I noted in the preceding chapter, your valleys can be perfect opportunities for starting anew.

And, Finally, Make Your Move

When you do, you're sure to make the most of your life.

About the Author

JIMMY CALANO founded the international training company CareerTrack in 1982. Just 10 years later, it had become one of the world's largest purveyors of professional development audio, video, and seminar-style training programs.

CareerTrack achieved market leadership with its affordable tuition fees, unique training formats, and breakthrough direct-marketing strategies. The organization grew to 700 employees and $82 million in revenue, and conducted business in 24 countries. After presiding over CareerTrack for 13 years, Calano sold the company to a multinational corporation.

Jimmy is coauthor of *Real World 101* (Warner Books) and *CareerTracking* (Simon & Schuster). He lives in Boulder, Colorado, and enjoys reading, writing, speaking, spending time with his two children, and skiing Rocky Mountain powder as often as he can. You can reach him by e-mail at jcalano@aol.com.